Private
equity

Founded in 1807, John Wiley & Sons is the oldest independent publishing company in the United States. With offices in North America, Europe, Australia, and Asia, Wiley is globally committed to developing and marketing print and electronic products and services for our customers' professional and personal knowledge and understanding.

The Wiley Finance series contains books written specifically for finance and investment professionals as well as sophisticated individual investors and their financial advisors. Book topics range from portfolio management to e-commerce, risk management, financial engineering, valuation, and financial instrument analysis, as well as much more.

For a list of available titles, please visit our web site at www.Wiley Finance.com.

Private equity

Transforming Public Stock to Create Value

HAROLD BIERMAN, JR.

John Wiley & Sons, Inc.

Published by John Wiley & Sons, Inc., Hoboken, New Jersey.
Published simultaneously in Canada.

For general information on our other products and services, or technical support,
please contact our Customer Care Department within the United States at 800-
762-2974, outside the United States at 317-572-3993 or fax 317-572-4002.

Wiley also publishes its books in a variety of electronic formats. Some content that
appears in print may not be available in electronic books.

For more information about Wiley products, visit our web site at www.wiley.com.

Library of Congress Cataloging-in-Publication Data:
Bierman, Harold.
  Private equity : transforming public stock to create value / Harold Bierman, Jr.
      p.   cm.
      ISBN 0-471-39292-8 (cloth : alk. paper)
    1. Corporations—Valuation.   2. Private equity.   3. Going private
  (Securities)   4. Corporations—Finance.   5. Leveraged buyouts.
  6. Venture capital.   I. Title.
      HG4028.V3 B445 2003
      338.6'041—dc21   2002013636

Printed in the United States of America.

10 9 8 7 6 5 4 3 2 1

contents

Public corporations have many different types of investors, each type having a different financial objective. The primary objective of private equity is that the stockholders are likely to have similar financial objectives and it is much easier for the corporation's financial strategies to be consistent with these objectives.

Private equity frequently is associated with a leveraged buyout. The equity ownership of a public corporation is changed to equity that is not traded in a public market. There are significant financial advantages and there are also operational advantages. For example, management frequently becomes an owner of a significant amount of the equity and thus the interests of management and the owners become more convergent. Most importantly, the common stockholders can directly and effectively affect the corporate financial decisions.

The concepts of this book are important to investors interested in increasing their rates of return on their investments, without increasing their risk and to management interested in supplementing their wages with a significant share of the firm's profitability.

Harold Bierman, Jr.
Cornell University
Ithaca, NY

acknowledgments

Bill Kidd, Jim Hauslein, and Hall Wendel, practitioners of the art of private equity, helped educate me.

Sy Smidt and Jerry Hass, co-authors in other books, developed many of the ideas contained in this book.

I thank Diane Sherman for her typing efforts through many drafts of this book.

CHAPTER 1

The Many Virtues
of Private Equity

For purposes of this book the term *private equity* refers to the common stock of a corporation where that common stock is held by a relatively few investors and is not traded on any of the conventional stock markets. Normally the senior managers of the firm hold a significant percentage of the firm's stock, and we will assume that is the situation in all the cases discussed in this book.

In practice, the term *private equity* is used in several different ways. There are private equity investment firms that direct their clients' funds into mutual funds or to other money managers. There are even private equity funds that invest directly into publicly owned corporations, usually concentrating the investments into a few corporations.

Venture capital is a form of private equity. In this book the use of the term will be restricted to the investment in the equity of corporations that are, or will soon be, not publicly owned. An exception is the case of a partial leveraged buyout (LBO). This is almost private equity but the firm is still publicly traded.

Megginson, Nash, and vanRadenborgh (1996) offer a review of the history of privatization. Jensen (1993) covers the general issue of corporate control. Kleiman (1988) studied and reports the gains from LBO types of transactions.

What are the advantages of private equity?

SIMPLICITY

Because there are no public equity investors the private equity firm's financial reporting requirements to all the relevant governmental entities are reduced. This simplifies management's responsibilities and results in transaction cost savings for the firm.

With private equity there are no requirements that management keep Wall Street informed of the firm's expected earnings and then provide an explanation of the actual earnings and why they differ from the expected earnings. Decisions are not affected by short term earnings and the anticipated stock market's reactions to the earnings; thus the firm's decision making may be improved.

The firm's board of directors can be chosen for effectiveness rather than appearances or public relations.

ALIGNMENT OF MANAGEMENT AND OWNERSHIP

With the average publicly held firm the interests of management and the firm's ownership are not always perfectly aligned. An entire area of study called agency theory has been created with the objectives of studying and reducing the conflicts between a firm's management and its owners. The classic papers on agency theory are Jensen and Meckling (1976) and Jensen (1986).

We assume the common stock of the private equity firm discussed in this book is to a significant extent owned by management. Management has an incentive to act in a manner consistent with maximizing the well-being of the equity owners.

DIVIDEND POLICY OF A PRIVATE EQUITY FIRM

The owners of a private equity firm tend to be paid for their services as members of management, consultants, or members of the firm's board of directors. They also hope for a value accretion to their stock holdings.

If the owners are also employees of the firm, the incomes earned for services will be taxed at ordinary income tax rates. But there is only one level of tax since the corporation gets a tax deduction for the amounts paid for service. This is the first tax advantage.

The gain from the value accretion of the stock will be taxed in the future at a capital gains rate when the gain is realized for tax purposes. Thus there are two tax advantages from value accretion and the use of private equity; one is tax deferral and the second is the lower capital gains tax rate compared to the tax rate on ordinary income.

The private equity firm has little or no incentive to pay cash dividends on the common stock. The investors would rather be paid as employees or have their equity investment gains be converted into capital gains and have these gains taxed at the lower capital gains tax rate in the future.

CAPITAL STRUCTURE

The normal public corporation has managers and owners. While the managers may also be stockholders, the total value of their stock investment in the corporation tends to be much less than the present value of their salaries and bonuses. The senior managers of public corporations have a significant incentive to act in such a way as to not jeopardize the stream of salaries that will be earned if the managers are not dislodged from their jobs.

With a private equity firm the relative values of salaries and ownership are changed. Now the owners have an incentive to substitute debt for equity both to gain (or maintain) control and to add value. The use of debt becomes a much more important tool for adding value with a private equity firm than with a public firm.

VENTURE CAPITAL

This is not a book on venture capital though many of the conclusions of this book apply equally to venture capital activities, since venture capital is a form of private equity.

It is assumed in this book that the firm being taken private has a track record and its value can be estimated based on objective financial measures of the results of operations. Frequently, a venture capitalist is evaluating the story told by an entrepreneur. While there may be projected financial results, they frequently are not backed up by actual results. The valuation of such a firm is more an art than a science.

MBOs

DeAngelo and DeAngelo (1987) review the early history of managerial buyouts (MBOs). From 1973–1982 they identify 64 buyout proposals made by managers of New York and American Stock Exchange listed firms. They identify eight factors that are important in the decision to effect a management buyout. These are:

1. Potential improvement in managerial incentives
2. Save costs of disseminating information to stockholders
3. Company secrets are better protected
4. Tax savings of interest tax shields and other tax savings
5. Avoidance of hostile takeovers
6. Difficulty to raise capital
7. Illiquid stock (leading to greater difficulty attracting managers)
8. Disagreements among stockholders (because of illiquid investments)

Diamond (1985) put together a team of practitioners of the LBO art to construct a book that explores the legal, tax, accounting, operational, and financial considerations of an LBO transaction. It is a handy reference book regarding the practical aspects of the LBO deal.

THE J.P. MORGAN CHASE FUND

In February 2001 J.P. Morgan Chase announced that its J.P. Morgan Partners unit was raising $13 billion for a private equity fund (see the *Wall Street Journal* of February 6, 2001). While $8 billion was to be the bank's own funds, $5 billion was to be raised from other investors. These investors were to include pension funds, university endowments, and foundations. This fund raising effort followed the creation within a few months of Thomas Lee's $6.1 billion buyout fund and KKR's raising of a $6 billion fund.

Private equity funds primarily invest in leveraged buyouts but they are not precluded from investing in venture capital activities. Their main investment destination is the LBO but private equity investment can take many different forms.

J.P. Morgan Chase and its predecessors investing in private equity had earned a 40 percent annual return on equity capital. To evaluate this return we would need to know the amount of debt and other senior securities used, as well as the status and age of deals that have been undertaken, but are not yet completed (thus there is not yet an objective measurable internal rate of return). Also, the 40 percent return was earned on a smaller amount of capital than was now being raised. Investing a large sum of capital in firms of larger size has its own set of challenges for a private equity operation. The number of eligible targets is reduced. On the other hand the number of firms competing for those larger targets is also reduced.

CONCLUSIONS

There are several reasons why value may be added by a firm converting from being organized as a publicly owned firm to be a private equity firm. First, there are operational reasons why a private equity firm may have more value. Second, two financial decisions (dividends and capital structure) are likely to be different with a private equity firm than with a publicly owned firm. The set of financial decisions with the private equity firm is likely to add value to the investors owning the stock.

QUESTIONS AND PROBLEMS

1. What are the advantages of private equity?

2. Of the eight factors listed by DeAngelo and DeAngelo, which one do you consider most important?

3a. Assume the LBO management firm is paid 2 percent on Company B's total assets and 20 percent of the gross profits (before capital charges and after taxes). The capital structure for Company B is:

	Dollars
Debt (.14)	$40
Preferred (.12)	30
Convertible preferred (.06)	20
Equity	10

Company B has a .35 tax rate. It earned $90 before interest before taxes before management charges.

Required: Allocate the $90.

3b. Now assume the firm earns $45 before interest, taxes, and management changes.

Required: Allocate the $45.

CHAPTER 2

Valuing the Target Firm

Aside from venture capital situations and restructuring efforts, private equity capital firms tend to invest in either a leveraged buyout (LBO) or a management buyout (MBO). Either of these two buyouts (differing only to the extent of the magnitude of management's participation in the new equity split) may be facilitated by a merchant bank, which would supply some of the equity capital and possibly other types of capital. Merchant bankers or their equivalent have to set a value on the firm that is being converted to a private equity capital firm.

The valuation of a firm for the purpose being discussed is analogous to the familiar capital budgeting type of problem, but differs in several ways. Usually the target firm has a track record of generating cash flows; thus there is a sound objective basis for estimating the future cash flows. Secondly, the people buying the equity of a firm distrust a process that relies excessively on the forecast of the future cash flows. While any valuation process implicitly is forecasting the future cash flows, the extent of the forecasting may be less obvious when the buyer is using some calculation techniques compared to other techniques. Of course, when the buyer is computing the valuation of a firm, the current owners of the firm are also computing the value. If the buyer computes the firm's value to be larger than the seller's estimate, the likelihood of a sale of the firm increases.

First, we consider a value measure that is completely objective and then we review measures that become more and more subjective.

MARKET CAPITALIZATION

In some situations the only completely objective value measure is the market capitalization. This is equal to the number of outstanding shares of common stock times the market price per share, assuming the market price is observable and there are no complexities in computing the number of outstanding shares. Any acquirer would have to expect to pay a premium to the current market capitalization. The market value of the common stock sets a floor for an offering price by a buyer. Rarely would a buyer consider submitting a bid less than current market price and expect to acquire a majority of the outstanding shares. In fact, one would expect the acquirer to have to pay a premium over the market price. Thus the market price of the common stock is an important measure of value since it sets a minimum-offering price.

It can be argued that, with a closely held corporation, if the stockholders desire to unload their stock, they may not be able to, because the market is too thin. In such a situation the seller might accept the market price or even marginally less than the market price, since the market price does not fairly represent the firm's value.

Can one obtain the value of the stockholders' equity by using the market value for a few shares traded on the stock market? It should be remembered that the entire universe of investors is available as possible purchasers of the stock and that the present owners are not bidding up the stock price to acquire more shares. Normally it will not take a large price increase to cause the present investors to sell their shares of stock assuming the price before the bid was set by the market. Premiums paid by the acquirers in most deals are less than .30.

MULTIPLIERS

The use of multipliers for valuation is common practice. A multiplier is applied to some type of flow measure. The multiplier is frequently based on the observed relationships of comparable firms. The following multipliers are used:

■ Price-earnings multiplier.
■ Cash flow multiplier (EBITDA and free cash flow multipliers).
EBITDA is earnings before interest, taxes, depreciation, and amortization.
Free cash flow is cash flow from operations after maintenance capital expenditures. Sometimes free cash flow is computed after all investment outlays.
■ Cash flow multipliers applied to the next period's flows (e.g., NEBITDA).

If one takes the current earnings and multiplies by the current price-earnings multiplier, one obtains the current market price. The expected earnings of the current year or an adjusted earnings can be used rather than the observed earnings of the past year. Another variation is to use the expected earnings of the next year.

The use of the expected earnings times a price-earnings multiplier is a common technique for evaluating prospective acquisitions. It may be a shortcut method of applying discounted cash flows. The following mathematical model illustrates this position.

Let P = the market price per share
k = the discount rate
g = the growth rate in earnings and dividends
E = the earnings
b = the retention percentage
$(1 - b)E$ = dividends

Since

$$P = \frac{(1-b)E}{k-g}$$

we can divide both sides by E and obtain:

$$P/E = \frac{(1-b)}{k-g}$$

The price-earnings ratio (*P/E*) that is expected is equal to the dividend payout rate (1 – *b*) divided by *k* – *g*. The larger the value of the growth rate (*g*), the larger the value of the *P/E* ratio that will be justified.

Assume the *P/E* of comparable firms is computed to be 8 and the earnings to the stockholders of the target firm are $10,000,000. The valuation of the stock is $80,000,000. But the following complexities exist:

- Were the other firms really comparable?
- Were the earnings really $10,000,000 or should adjustments be made?
- Does the firm have excess assets?
- Does the firm have unrecorded liabilities?
- Is there reason to expect that next year's earnings will differ significantly from $10,000,000?
- Is the average *P/E* of 8 for comparable firms reasonable?

Instead of using an earnings multiplier many merchant bankers prefer to use a cash flow (or EBITDA or free cash flow) multiplier. Again the multiplier is obtained from observing comparable firms. Assume the cash flow (EBITDA) multiplier of comparable firms is 6 and the firm's cash flow (EBITDA) is $20,000,000. Now the firm's estimated value is $120,000,000. If the debt is $40,000,000 this value is consistent with the $80,000,000 value of the stockholders' position obtained previously. The value normally obtained using EBITDA is the firm's value (debt plus equity) rather than the stockholders' value.

Now let us consider the average *P/E* of 8 for 10 comparable firms. Assume that 9 firms have a *P/E* of 5 and one firm has a *P/E* of 35.

$$\text{Ave } P/E = \frac{9(5) + 1(35)}{10} = \frac{80}{10} = 8$$

The harmonic average takes an average of the reciprocals and then takes the reciprocal of the average.

$$\text{Ave of reciprocals} = \frac{1}{10}\left[\left(\frac{1}{5}\right)9 + \left(\frac{1}{35}\right)1\right]$$

$$= \frac{1}{10}\left(\frac{9}{5} + \frac{1}{35}\right) = \frac{1}{10}\left(\frac{64}{35}\right) = \frac{6.4}{35}$$

$$\text{Reciprocal} = \frac{35}{6.4} = 5.47$$

Is a *P/E* of 8 or 5.47 the correct average for purposes of computing the firm's value?

The conventional average (the *P/E* of 8) tends to weight extreme values higher than is appropriate. For example, assume there are 3 comparable firms, 2 with *P/E*s of 10 and 1 with a *P/E* of 100. The conventional average *P/E* is 40.

$$\text{Average } P/E = \frac{2(10) + 1(100)}{3} = \frac{120}{3} = 40$$

The harmonic average is $14^2/_7$:

$$\text{Average of reciprocals} = \frac{1}{3}\left(\frac{2}{10} + \frac{1}{100}\right) = \frac{21}{300}$$

$$\text{Reciprocals} = \frac{300}{21} = 14^2/_7$$

It is not obvious that 40 is the correct measure. The example could be more extreme by having the *P/E* of the third firm 10,000 (as might occur if earnings were unusually low for the observed year). The average *P/E* is

$$\text{Ave } P/E = \frac{2(10) + 1(10,000)}{3} = \frac{10,020}{3} = 3,340$$

It is not obvious that a P/E of 3,340 would lead to a sensible value measure. The harmonic average is

$$\text{Ave of reciprocals } = \frac{1}{3}\left(\frac{2}{10} + \frac{1}{10,000}\right) = \frac{2,001}{30,000}$$

$$\text{Reciprocals } = \frac{30,000}{2,001} = 14.99$$

The 14.99 P/E multiplier would seem to be more useful for valuation purposes than the 3,340 P/E multiplier.

Multipliers: Theoretical Basis

The use of the average P/E of comparable firms has the complexities of determining firms that are actually comparable and computing the average P/E. An alternative approach is to compute a theoretical target P/E based on the firm's economic characteristics. We will consider three different multipliers, all of which will be used to compute the value of the stock.

M_0 applied to after-tax earnings: $M_0(E)$
M_1 applied to earnings before interest and taxes: $M_1(EBIT)$
M_2 applied to earnings before interest, taxes, depreciation, and amortization: $M_2(EBITDA)$

Determination of M_0

Let P be the value now of a share of common stock. Then by definition of M_0:

$$P = M_0 E$$

or

$$M_0 = \frac{P}{E}$$

Let P = the value of the stock
E = the earnings of the stock
D = the dividend
k = the cost of equity
g = the growth ratio of earnings and dividend

If $P = \dfrac{D}{k-g}$ then the theoretical value of the earnings multiplier is:

$$M_0 = \frac{D}{E(k-g)} = \frac{(1-b)E}{E(k-g)} = \frac{1-b}{k-g}$$

If we know the values of b, k, and g then we can compute the value of the multiplier (M_0) that can be used to compute the value of the stock.

Let E = $65, D = $39, k = .12, g = .02

$$E - D = 26, \; b = \frac{26}{65} = .4, \; \text{EBIT} = \$100, \; \text{EBITDA} = \$150$$

Then

$$P = \frac{39}{.12 - .02} = \$390$$

and

$$M_0 = \frac{1-b}{k-g} = \frac{.6}{.12 - .02} = 6$$

and

$$P = M_0 E = 6(65) = \$390$$

Determination of M_1

M_1 is the multiplier of EBIT where

$$(1 - t)\text{EBIT} = E$$

if there is no debt.

$$P = \frac{D}{k - g} = \frac{(1 - b)E}{k - g} = \frac{(1 - b)(1 - t)\text{EBIT}}{k - g}$$

Since

$$P = M_1(\text{EBIT})$$

$$M_1 = \frac{(1 - b)(1 - t)}{k - g}$$

For the example, if $t = .35$

$$M_1 = \frac{.6(.65)}{.10} = 3.9$$

and since EBIT = $100:

$$P = M_1(\text{EBIT}) = 3.9(100) = \$390$$

The value of the common stock is again $390.

Determination of M_2

M_2 is the multiplier using EBITDA that can be used to compute P.
  Define EBITDA in terms of EBIT.

  EBITDA = q(EBIT)
  For the example $q = 1.5$
  EBITDA = $1.5(100) = 150$

Since

$$P = M_2(\text{EBITDA}) = \frac{(1 - b)(1 - t)\text{EBIT}}{k - g}$$

and

$$(\text{EBITDA}) = q(\text{EBIT})$$

$$P = \frac{(1-b)(1-t)(\text{EBITDA})}{(k-g)q}$$

and

$$M_2 = \frac{(1-b)(1-t)}{(k-g)q} = \frac{.6(.65)}{.10(1.5)} = 2.6$$

Thus

$$P = 2.6(150) = \$390$$

Remember the above example assumes zero debt. With outstanding debt the formulation becomes more complex.

The above multipliers cannot be applied to a different firm with a different cost of equity and a different growth rate. The multipliers were computed based on specific information, and other information will lead to different multipliers.

Since all the above measures are based on objective measures of earnings, EBIT and EBITDA, they appear to be objective, but in fact all the calculations have a significant subjective input. However, the appearance of objectivity makes them popular methods of valuation.

Since all the methods are implicitly assuming future benefits, it is sensible to also compute the present value of these benefits.

MEASURES OF PRESENT VALUE

We consider six different present value calculations that are actually all equivalent, thus are actually one method:

1. Present value of future dividends for perpetuity
2. Present value of discretionary (free) cash flows

3. Present value of future earnings minus the present value of new investments
4. Present value of an earnings perpetuity plus the present value of growth opportunities (PVGO)
5. Present value of dividends for n years plus present value of the firm's value at time n
6. Present value of economic incomes

For the infinite life situation with the firm earning $65 and paying $39 of dividends, a .12 cost of equity and a .02 growth rate, the value is:

$$P = \frac{D}{k-g} = \frac{39}{.12 - .02} = \$390$$

Define the present value of growth opportunities (PVGO) to be:

$$PVGO = \frac{E(g - bk)}{k(k-g)} = \frac{65[.02 - .4(.12)]}{.12(.12 - .02)} = -\$151.67$$

The value of the stock is:

$$P = \frac{E}{k} + PVGO = \frac{65}{.12} - 151.67 = \$390$$

The firm is retaining .4 of earnings and has a growth rate of .02. This implies that incremental investments earn .05. Since .05 is less than the cost of equity, the undertaking of the growth opportunities actually reduces value.

Instead of assuming one growth rate for perpetuity one could assume a series of changing growth rates. The calculations and formulations are more complex, but the logic is perfectly consistent with the infinite life and one growth rate model.

Reinvestment Rate Greater than the Cost of Equity

Now assume all facts are the same except the firm earns .15 on new investments and has a .06 growth rate (.4 of earnings are retained).

$$P = \frac{D}{k-g} = \frac{39}{.12-.06} = \$650$$

The equity value is now $650. The present value of growth opportunities is $108.33.

$$PVGO = \frac{E(g-bk)}{k(k-g)} = \frac{65[.06-.4(.12)]}{.12(.12-.06)} = \frac{65(.012)}{.0072} = \$108.33$$

The value of the stock is:

$$P = \frac{E}{K} + PVGO = \frac{65}{.12} + 108.33 = \$650$$

Finite Life Models

To illustrate the finite life models we will use a three-year time horizon. The projected net cash flows are

1.	$11,000
2.	10,890
3.	10,648
Terminal Value	66,550

With a .10 cost of equity using the above cash flows the firm's value at time 0 (V_0) is:

$$V_0 = \frac{11,000}{1.10} + \frac{10,890}{(1.10)^2} + \frac{77,198}{(1.10)^3} = 10,000 + 9,000 + 58,000$$
$$= \$77,000$$

For simplification assume there are no taxes. Assume the four balance sheets are as shown in Table 2.1.

The economic incomes for the three years are as shown in Table 2.2.

$PV (.10) = -\$18,154$ (PV of economic incomes)
PV of residual value $= 66,555(1.10)^{-3} = 50,000$
PV of terminal book value $= 73,000(1.10)^{-3} = 54,846$

The firm's value is:

V_0 = book value + PV of incomes + PV of residual value
    $- PV$ of terminal book value
$V_0 = 100,000 - 18,154 + 50,000 - 54,846 = \$77,000$

The present values of the economic incomes plus the initial book value plus the present value of the residual value minus the present value of the terminal book value is equal to the firm's value at time 0. The amount is also equal to the present value of the cash flows.

TABLE 2.1 Four Balance Sheets

	Time 0	1	2	3 (before adjustment)
Assets	100,000	91,000	82,000	73,000
Stock Equity	100,000	91,000	82,000	73,000

TABLE 2.2 Economic Incomes

	1	2	3
Revenues	11,000	10,890	10,648
Depreciation	9,000	9,000	9,000
Interest	10,000	9,100	8,200
Economic Income	-8,000	-7,210	-6,552

FREE CASH FLOW

If free cash flow is defined to be equal to the cash flows as defined (after all investments), then there are no complexities. The preceding calculations apply.

If the free cash flow is after maintenance cap-ex, but is not equal to the preceding cash flows, both sets of calculations would require adjustment to reflect the additional investments.

CHANGING THE CAPITAL STRUCTURE

If the people valuing the firm intend to substitute debt for equity, then the changes in capital structure can give rise to an increase in value. This potential increase in value is discussed in Chapter 5.

EARNINGS VERSUS DIVIDENDS VERSUS CASH FLOWS: PRESENT VALUE CALCULATIONS

Assume the objective is to compute the value of a firm using present value calculations. Should earnings be used? Since earnings fail to consider the funds necessary to be reinvested to generate future earnings, earnings cannot be used without adjusting for reinvestment or alternatively using the present value of economic incomes illustrated previously in this chapter.

The risk-adjusted present value of future dividends is a theoretically correct method of computing the value of a firm's stock equity, if dividends are defined to include all cash flowing from the firm to the stockholders, whatever the form of the flow. Despite the correctness of using dividends, there are complexities. First, the amount of dividends is a derived measure. It is derived from the projections of future cash flows or earnings of the firm. Second, in a situation where there are no cash dividends it is very difficult (but not impossible) to estimate the future dividends. Third, an acquirer tends to be more comfortable with the use of the target firm's cash flows or earnings. Where the target firm is paying a dividend, the difficult estimation problem is to determine the growth rate for perpetuity. An alternative calculation is to estimate the growth for n years and multiply the dividend at time n by a multiplier to represent the firm's value at that time. Since the target firm's dividend is likely to be changed (or eliminated) after the restructuring, the dividend calculation is likely to be viewed as misleading.

ESTIMATION PROBLEMS

If the economic incomes as illustrated are used to compute value, then the various accounting conventions do not affect the value measure. It appears that the initial book value and the allocation of costs to time periods affect the value calculation using earnings, but the appearances are misleading. Among the accounting conventions that do not affect the theoretical value calculation adjustment are:

- Depreciation method
- Expensing or capitalizing of expenses (including R&D)
- Write-off or not of goodwill

Income with a multiplier cannot be used easily if:

- The firm has a loss or very small income compared to assets.
- The firm has a large amount of noncash utilizing expenses (goodwill and depreciation expense) compared to income.
- The accounting income measure is not reliable.
- There are extra assets recorded or not recorded.
- There are unrecorded or recorded excess liabilities.

For any method where the future benefits are being discounted to the present there are the problems of determining the discount rate and estimating the growth rate.

If the firm is not investing any of the earnings, then dividends equal the earnings and there is not likely to be large expected growth. This simplifies the value calculation but also is likely to result in a lower valuation, compared to a growth situation.

BUYING FOR LIQUIDATION

In some situations a target firm is acquired so that it can be liquidated. In 1988 American Brands Corporation acquired E-II Holdings, Inc. for $1.1 billion plus the assumption of E-II's debt. It acquired 18 different operating units plus 7.1 million shares of its own stock (with a value of $320 million). American immediately sold nine of the units for $950 million of cash (plus $250 million of preferred stock that was worth very little), plus the E-II debt was assumed by the buyer. In acquiring E-II an important consideration for American Brands was how much it would be able to obtain for the units to be sold. It also wanted to purchase its own shares and repel a raid. American Brands was employing a Pac-Man strategy. Since E-II acquired American shares, American acquired E-II. E-II's probable intention was to liquidate American (American consisted of tobacco, office products, liquor, and financial services).

CONCLUSIONS

Valuation is very much an art. This is particularly true when the firm does not have a long history of earnings and cash flows.

The difficult part of valuing a firm is to obtain reasonable estimates of future cash flows or earnings, but it is important that once these measures are obtained they be summarized correctly.

There are a variety of measures all with some highly subjective element that can be used by the decision makers in attempting to determine the value of a firm. There are exact methods of calculation, but there are not exact reliable measures of value.

The going concern value of the assets, with the assets gaining their value from the cash flow, is the relevant measure. The prime advantage to be gained by using cash flow versus conventional income is that it is theoretically correct and it does not tie us to the results of accounting procedures that are not designed for this specific type of decision. If the decision makers want to use the current income as the basis for making their investment decision, care should be taken, since the computation may not be equivalent to the use of cash flows. However, even if they do not use the income measure directly, the decision makers will use it indirectly as the basis for their evaluation of future dividends.

Remember that in no case is the value determined by calculating the present value of the accounting earnings. This calculation is not theoretically correct. The present value of economic incomes can be used, as long as the initial book value, ending book value, and terminal value are all included in the calculation.

But even when the firm has a long history, there is always the question of whether there has been a significant change in the business environment; thus the firm's past history may not give a good indication of the firm's future performance.

In many situations the verbal description of the reasons why the firm has value is more relevant for valuation than a value derived from growth rate assumptions that cannot be adequately justified.

In conclusion, you should do calculations, but fully describe the assumptions, the basis of the assumptions, and also estimate the value of the firm if these assumptions are not valid.

QUESTIONS AND PROBLEMS

1. Which is a more reliable estimate of value, market capitalization or the present value of the firm's future cash flows?

2. The price-earnings multiplier for comparable firms is a popular method of valuation. When would this valuation method not be reliable?

3. In the chapter we have: $P/E = \dfrac{(1-b)}{k-g}$

   If the firm has a low retention rate and a large growth rate what does this imply?

   Would you expect a high or low P/E ratio?

4. One can multiply a constant (multiplier) times a firm's EBITDA. Explain what one gets from the product.

5. Assume the value of a firm is: $P = \dfrac{D}{k-g} = \dfrac{50}{.12-.10} = \$2,500$

   The firm uses zero debt. The retention rate is .60.

   What is the earnings return on new investment?

   What is the value of the firm's PVGO?

CHAPTER 3

Structuring and Selling the Deal

The first step in creating private equity is to value the target firm (see Chapter 2). The second step is to structure the financing so that the securities can be sold to the relevant types of capital contributors.

Capital financing fashions for private equity firms have changed. In the 1980s an acquirer could finance the acquisition with as much as 99 percent debt and preferred stock. In the new millennium that acquirer would be very lucky to get debt money for 50 percent of the needed capital. The sources of capital range from common stock to pure debt with many types of hybrids in between. Stern and Chew (1998) give a good summary of the private equity revolution.

SOURCES OF CAPITAL

- Debt: equity capital firms, banks, pension funds, seller of firm
- Debt with equity kicker: same as above and add insurance companies and rich people
- Preferred stock: insurance companies
- Convertible preferred stock: insurance companies or other corporations
- Common stock: LBO or private equity firms, LBO funds, and rich people

BID FOR ACQUISITION

Assume there are no agency costs and no costs of financial distress. The objective of the private equity buyers is to maximize the net value.

Let Assets = the total value of the firm including any outstanding debt, but before new debt

Bid = the amount of the bid for the firm

B_o = outstanding debt assumed by new corporation

V_L = equal to cash raised by debt issue to finance acquisition

t = the corporate tax rate

S = the value of equity before refinancing

where

$$S = \text{Assets} - B_o$$

and the net to the equity investor with no new debt issued by the firm but the B_o debt assumed is:

$$\text{Net} = S - \text{Bid}$$

But assume V_L of maximum new debt is issued

where t = the corporate tax rate:

$$V_L = S + tV_L$$

and

$$V_L = \frac{S}{1-t}$$

Now the new net to the equity investor is:

$$\text{Net} = \frac{S}{1-t} - \text{Bid} = V_L - \text{Bid}$$

and the new debt proceeds minus the amount bid is the net value to the investor (if maximum debt is issued, the value of the firm's stock is zero).

Since Bid is set, the larger the value of V_L (the value of the leveraged firm), the larger the value of the equity of the investors (though the value of the firm's stock equals zero). The investors receive cash or the debt being issued.

Example 1

$$t = .35, \ S = \text{Assets} = \$650,000, \text{ no initial debt}$$

$$V_L = \frac{650,000}{1-.35} = \$1,000,000$$

Assume $700,000 is Bid and $1,000,000 of the debt is issued.

$$V_L = \$1,000,000$$

$$\text{Net} = V_L - B$$

$$\text{Net} = \$1,000,000 - 700,000 = \$300,000$$

The $1,000,000 of debt proceeds are given to the new shareholders and they pay $700,000 for the firm.

The net gain is $300,000. This is the largest feasible Net and $1,000,000 is the largest V_L that is feasible, without other sources of values. The maximization of V_L is consistent with the maximization of the buyer's value. The firm is being financed with 100 percent debt.

Realistically less than maximum debt ($1,000,000) will be issued and the net gain will be less than $300,000, unless there are improvements in operations.

Example 2

Same assumptions as Example 1 but the firm (with Assets = $650,000) initially has S = $260,000 and B_o = $390,000.

If the maximum amount of debt is issued, then $400,000 will be given to the shareholders.

$$V_L = \frac{S}{1-t} = \frac{260,000}{.65} = \$400,000$$

Assuming a $270,000 bid for the equity, the net gain to the shareholders after the issuance of the debt is $130,000.

For the first example the bid was $50,000 larger than the initial stock value, but $1,000,000 of the debt was issued.

For the second example, the bid was $10,000 larger than the initial stock value but only $400,000 of the debt was issued (there is already $390,000 of debt outstanding).

In the second example we assumed the firm's assets had a value of $650,000. This number is normally hard to determine accurately and is apt to be the measure that gives rise to a deal's being done. The buyer and seller are likely to have different expectations and estimates of value.

STRUCTURING A DEAL

To simplify the presentation we assume that the acquisition will be financed by a mix of debt and common stock and that no other types of capital are feasible.

There are two primary issues to be resolved:

1. The split between debt and equity
2. The percentage of equity to be kept by the deal's promoter and the percentage to be given to the other equity contributors

Generally there is a maximum amount of debt that banks and other debt sources are willing to provide. This maximum changes through time but promoters of private equity deals normally have a good idea of this maximum. The normal amount of debt can be increased by adding an equity kicker to the debt security. This kicker may be in the form of a conversion feature, warrants on stock, or a bonus based on the firm's future earnings or cash flows. But there must be recognition that the nominal amount of hybrid debt of this nature is not all debt but a mix of debt and equity.

The percentage of the equity to be given to the other equity providers must result in an expected internal rate of return (IRR) that is large enough to attract the equity. This implies that it is necessary to estimate the firm's future value and split the value among all the capital contributors so that each investor class can compute the return that is expected to be earned and be pleased with that return.

An Example

Assume that a firm can be acquired for $78,000,000 and the expected cash-out date is three years. The firm's value at that time (the sale price) is estimated to be $162,400,000. The underlying internal rate of return (IRR) of the firm is

$$78(1 + IRR)^3 = 162.4$$
$$IRR = .2769$$

The firm's underlying IRR of .2769 is reasonably impressive. But assume $60,000,000 of debt costs .18 and that the payment of the debt at time 3 would be $98,600,000.

$$60,000,000(1.18)^3 = \$98,600,000$$

Since the proceeds at time 3 from the sale of the firm are expected to be $162,400,000 the return to the equity contributors is $63,800,000.

$$162,400,000 - 98,600,000 = \$63,800,000$$

The equity contributors of $18,000,000 earn

$$18(1 + IRR)^3 = 63.8$$
$$IRR = .525$$

Assume the equity contributors of $17,000,000 want a return of .35 (the promoters contribute $1,000,000).
The $17,000,000 requires proceeds of $41,800,000 at time 3.

$$17(1.35)^3 = \$41.8 \text{ million}$$

This leaves $22,000,000 for the promoters.

$$63,800,000 - 41,800,000 = \$22,000,000$$

The promoters expect to earn an IRR of 1.8 or 180 percent on their $1,000,000 investment.

$$1(1 + IRR)^3 = 22$$
$$IRR = 1.80 \text{ or } 180\% \text{ per year}$$

With the given assumptions, the equity contributors of $17,000,000 to earn their .35 per year have to be awarded .655 of the equity.

$$\frac{41.8}{63.8} = .655$$

The promoters receive .345 of the equity and contribute $\frac{1}{18}$ or .056 of the equity capital.
Now assume that only $38,000,000 of .18 debt can be raised (rather than $60,000,000). At time 3 the debt payment will be $38,000,000(1.18)^3 = \$62,400,000$ and the stockholders will net $100,000,000.

$$162,400,000 - 62,400,000 = \$100,000,000$$

While this is larger than the $63,800,000 previously available, the amount of equity investment is now increased to $40,000,000. The $39,000,000 of external equity now requires $96,000,000 at time 3 to earn .35.

$$39(1.35)^3 = \$96.0 \text{ million}$$

This leaves $4,000,000 of return at time 3 for the promoters. The promoters investing $1,000,000 now earn an internal rate of return of .587.

$$1(1 + IRR)^3 = 4$$
$$IRR = .587$$

The promoters' IRR is reduced from 1.80 to .587 as a result of reducing the amount of debt. The equity split is now .96 for the new equity suppliers and .04 for the promoters (down from .345).

With the facts as given, the more debt at a cost of .18 the better for the promoters. However, we can expect the cost of debt to increase as debt is substituted for equity; thus generalizations are not feasible. The promoters must determine the cost of debt for the different amounts of debt. Also, the equity return requirements must be determined since the cost of equity capital will change as the percentage of debt capital is changed. Asquith and Wizman (1990) give data regarding bondholder returns in leveraged buyouts.

To simplify the presentation, we have assumed zero taxes. If taxes are included the analysis must consider the fact that interest is tax deductible each time period, thus will change the firm's terminal value if there is reinvestment of the savings.

Some analysts predict the equity value at the end of the planning horizon independent of the capital structure. This is faulty since the equity value is affected by the capital structure. The model illustrated assumed zero taxes and made no interim cash outlays to the capital contributors; thus the firm's value at time 3 is affected by operations and not by the capital structure decisions.

Obviously the promoter would like to keep as large a percentage of ownership as is feasible. The percentage is limited by the firm's prospects (the terminal value), the amount of debt that can be raised, and the costs (required expected returns) of the debt and other common stock investors. The percentage of ownership that is kept by the promoters is the residual results of the requirements of the investors that the promoters are trying to attract.

SELLING THE DEAL

For making capital budgeting decisions the net present value method has several advantages over the use of the IRR method. While the two methods will frequently lead to the same decision, there are also situations where they lead to different decisions unless they are carefully used.

In the present context the objective of the promoters is to sell a deal to investors, and the easiest measure to understand and persuade potential investors is an internal rate of return. It is more impressive to be told the IRR over a three year period is .587 than that the NPV is $626,000 (for the promoters) when the debt amount is $38,000,000 and the equity is $40,000,000.

A Partial LBO

The conventional LBO buys 100 percent of the common stock. If management is part of the LBO group, it will own a significant percentage of the private equity capital. The main problems are raising the private equity and accomplishing the LBO without attracting competition.

Now assume management has a different strategy. The corporation will repurchase its own shares. The stockholders who want cash receive it by selling some of their stock and having the gain on the stock sale taxed at a capital gains rate.

Assume that management currently owns or has rights (options) to 20 percent of the firm's 1,000,000 outstanding shares. The firm repurchases 30 percent of the 1,000,000 outstanding shares. There are 700,000 shares outstanding after the share repurchase. If management does not sell any of their shares, they will now own 28.57 percent of the shares (before the buyback they owned 20 percent).

$$\frac{200,000}{700,000} = .2857$$

Obviously, if the firm continues the buyback strategy, and if management does not sell any of its shares, its percentage of ownership will increase. In a few years management will have the same percentage of ownership that it would have obtained with an immediate LBO. An important advantage of the partial LBO strategy is that management's investment is highly liquid compared to an investment in a LBO. We will discuss this strategy in greater depth in Chapter 9.

CONCLUSIONS

After valuing the target firm and deciding on the amount to be bid there remains the decision to split the capital needs among the different forms of capital. In this chapter we limit the choice to either debt or equity. The next calculation is to determine the percentage of equity that must be allocated to the external investors so that the investors can expect to earn the return they require given the alternative returns available, the risks of the enterprise being financed, and the amount of debt (and other senior securities) being issued.

It is important to remember that the amount (or value) of equity at the termination date will depend on the amount of debt being used.

QUESTIONS AND PROBLEMS

1. Why are insurance companies more likely to buy preferred stock than individuals?

2a. Assume the market capitalization of a firm's stock is $6,500,000 and there is $10,000,000 of debt outstanding. How much additional debt can be issued if the $6,500,000 is accepted as being reasonable? There is a .35 corporate tax rate.

2b. If a bid of $7,000,000 is made for the $6,500,000 of equity, how much can the buyers hope to make?

2c. With a bid of $7,000,000 and a cash-out of $12,243,000 after four years, the equity investors earn what IRR?

2d. Now assume $6,000,000 of .08 debt (zero coupon), zero taxes, and a cash-out of $12,243,000 minus debt payments at time 4. What IRR does the $1,000,000 of equity earn?

2e. Now assume a .35 tax rate. Compute the value at time 4 from reinvesting the tax savings to earn .08 before tax and .08(1 − .35) = .052 after tax.

2f. What IRR is earned on the equity capital of $1,000,000? Assume the $12,243,000 from (2c.) is after tax except for the tax savings from the debt.

3. If equity investors contribute $1,000,000 and want a .30 return at time 4, how much do they require at time 4?

CHAPTER 4

A Changed Dividend Policy

A common stock dividend is a distribution of a portion of the assets of a corporation to its common stock shareholders. The amount received by an investor is proportional to the number of shares held. In most cases, cash is distributed. On rare occasions, a publicly held corporation may pay a dividend in a form other than cash. For example, a corporation may distribute, as a dividend, the shares it owns in another corporation. The Owens-Illinois Corporation did this as a means of complying with a court decree which required it to reduce its holdings of common stock in Owens–Corning Fiberglas.

When a corporation pays a dividend, its assets are reduced by the amount of the dividend. In publicly traded stock, the price per share declines by approximately the amount of the dividend on the day that the stock goes ex-dividend. The owner of the stock, at the moment the stock goes ex-dividend, will receive the dividend. Because of other factors affecting the stock price, as well as tax considerations, the decline in the share price will be less than the amount of dividend paid.

DIVIDEND POLICY

A corporation is not legally obligated to declare a dividend of any specific amount. Thus, the board of directors actually has a specific decision every time a dividend is declared. However, once the Board declares a dividend, the corporation is legally obligated to make the payments. Therefore, a dividend should not be declared unless a corporation is in a financial position to make the payment.

The expectation of receiving dividends (broadly defined as any distribution of value) ultimately determines the market value of the common stock. By declaring a dividend, the board of directors is not only turning over some of the assets of the corporation to its stockholders, but it may be influencing the expectations stockholders have about the future dividends they can expect from the corporation. If expectations are affected, the dividend decision and the underlying dividend policy will have a short term impact on the value the market places on the common stock of the corporation.

Many financial experts believe that a highly stable but growing dividend is advantageous to a company. The most common reason stated for this belief is that stockholders prefer a steady income from their investments. There is at least one other important reason for thinking that a highly variable dividend rate may not be in the best interest of a company. In the long run, the value of a share of stock tends to be determined by the discounted value of the expected dividends. Insofar as this is the case, a widely fluctuating dividend rate will tend to make it difficult for stockholders to determine the value of the stock to them and as a result, the stock is likely to sell at a somewhat lower price than comparable stocks paying the same average dividend through time, but making the payments at a steady rate. This conclusion assumes investors are risk averse.

Reasons for Paying Dividends

There have been two rules of thumb with respect to dividend policy of publicly held corporations; first, that it is necessary for the firm to pay cash dividends to common stockholders and second, the dividends through time must increase. It is far from obvious that the above policies are optimum from the point of view of maximizing the well-being of stockholders. In this chapter we consider the effect of different dividend policies on the well-being of the common stockholders. Private equity capital offers complete flexibility regarding dividend policy.

The board of directors of an average publicly owned company knows that a significant percentage of its investors want dividends and others do not. Unfortunately, what the company knows is frequently wrong. With private equity capital the desires of the stockholders are more easily determined and their objectives are more likely to be identical. The private equity shareholders are likely to want capital gains and are likely to want these capital gains realized in the future, not realized now.

The primary reasons for paying dividends are:

- Zero tax investors (or low tax)
- Have done it in the past
- Trust legal list
- Few good investments (too much cash)
- Raiders
- Do right by investors (investors need cash for consumption)

If investors do not pay taxes (or have a very low tax rate), then cash dividends are a sensible way of a corporation's distributing cash.

The argument that a corporation should increase its dividend payment because it has done so in the past finds its justification in the fact that investors wanting dividends would incur transaction costs switching investments if the policy were changed.

If a firm does not have good investment alternatives, it should consider a dividend. All investors have opportunity costs for money. They can invest the funds to earn an expected return consistent with what the market has to offer. The corporation should distribute the cash to its stockholders if it cannot invest it to beat the investor's opportunity cost.

The attitudes of investors are important factors to be considered. Consistently increasing dividends are generally welcomed by investors as indicators of profitability and safety. Uncertainty is increased by lack of dividends or dividends that fluctuate widely. Also dividends are thought to have an informational content; that is, an increase in dividends means that the board of directors expects the firm to do well in the future. Another important reason for the payment of dividends is that a wide range of investors need the dividends for consumption purposes. While such investors could sell a portion of their holdings, this latter transaction has relatively high transaction costs compared to cashing a dividend check. The presence of investors desiring cash for consumption makes it difficult to change the current dividend policy, even where such a change is dictated by the logic of the situation. Though one group of investors may benefit from a change in dividend policy, another group may be harmed. While we will see that income taxes tend to make a retention policy more desirable than cash dividends, the presence in the real world of zero tax and low tax investors dictates that we consider each situation individually and be flexible in arriving at a distribution policy.

Reasons for Not Paying Dividends

The motivations for not paying cash dividends are:

■ There are better forms of distribution than cash dividends, given tax considerations.
■ There are transaction costs with an investor receiving cash and then having to reinvest.
■ The firm has transaction costs if it needs to raise an equivalent amount of cash to substitute for the dividend.
■ Retention may be better than a dividend when the firm has good investments and the tax law favors retention compared to cash dividends.

The advantage of private equity is that the cash distribution decision can be made purely on the grounds of maximizing the value of the firm's common stock values.

Irrelevance of Dividend Policy

Let us assume that there are:

■ No transaction costs
■ No taxes

■ Informed rational investors
■ Investment policy set

Miller and Modigliani (1961) argue that with no income taxes and other well defined assumptions (such as perfect knowledge and certainty) a dollar retained is equal in value to a dollar distributed; thus dividend policy is not a relevant factor in determining the value of a corporation. However, when taxes are allowed in the analysis, dividend policy very much affects the value of the stockholders' equity. In practice, corporations appear to be influenced in setting dividend policy by the behavior of other corporations, and by a desire to have a relatively stable dividend.

The theoretical solution is for a corporation to invest in all desirable investments. If any cash is left over after the investments are made, the excess cash is distributed to the stockholders. In the real world, the dividend is frequently considered to be a firm obligation, and this obligation will affect the amount available for dividends.

Since private equity capital is most beneficial for investors in the higher tax brackets, we will assume for the investors a .396 tax rate on ordinary income and a .20 tax rate on long term capital gains.

The Value: One-Period Horizon

Assume a firm pays a $1 dividend and the investor nets after tax $(1 - t_p)$ and invests to earn an after tax return of r_p so that after one year the investor has:

$$(1 - t_p)(1 + r_p)$$

With retention by the corporation of the $1 where the corporation earns r and then pays a dividend the investor has:

$$(1 + r)(1 - t_p)$$

There is indifference for dividends and retention if $r = r_p$. If r is larger than r_p, then retention is better than an immediate dividend.

Assume $r_p = .0604$ and $r = .10$. We would expect retention to be better than an immediate dividend. Assume the firm has $100 available. With a dividend the investor has after one year:

$$100(1 - t_p)(1 + r_p) = 60.40(1.0604) = \$64.048$$

If the firm retains for one year and earns .10 and then pays a dividend, the investor has:

$$100(1.10)(1 - .396) = \$66.44$$

If the firm could earn only $r = r_p = .0604$, the investor would again have $64.048.

$$100(1.0604)(.604) = \$64.048$$

The relationships hold if there are n time periods instead of one. If $r = r_p$ there is indifference for dividends and retention. If the firm retains and does not pay a cash dividend, the required return is reduced if there is a capital gain.

The Value with a Dividend: Five-Year Horizon

Assume a firm has $100 that it can either invest or pay a dividend. The investor can earn a return of .0604 after investor tax on investments in the market.

The investor nets $60.40 after tax from the $100 dividend and after five years the investor who invests in the market will have $80.98:

$$60.40(1.0604)^5 = \$80.98$$

The Value with Retention and Sale

Now assume the firm reinvests the $100 for five years and earns .10 per year. After five years the firm will have $161.05:

$$100(1.10)^5 = \$161.05$$

Assume the firm is sold at time 5 for $161.05 and the investor is taxed at .20:

$$(1 - .20)(161.05) = \$128.84$$

This strategy is consistent with the manner in which private equity is managed. The advantage of the retention strategy compared to a dividend is $47.86 for the example or an increase of .59 above the future value with the annual dividend.

Most corporations have a mixed strategy of paying out a percentage of their earnings and retaining the remainder. Thus the actual difference in value for a typical dividend-paying corporation will not be as dramatic as for the example. But if we consider the change in value for the dividend component only, the example is accurate.

With the corporation retaining all the $100 of earnings the investor gives up $60.40 at time 0 and gets $128.84 at time 5. This is an IRR for the investor of .164.

$$60.40(1 + IRR)^5 = \$128.84$$
$$IRR = .164$$

The advantage of the retention strategy is highlighted by the fact that in a situation where the corporation can earn only .10 (after corporate tax and before investor tax), the investor earns .164 from the corporation after all taxes following a retention strategy rather than a dividend strategy.

Next, we want to consider the effect of lengthening the planning horizon from five years to 10 years.

A Ten-Year Horizon with Sale of Corporation

First assume the firm pays out the $100 as a dividend and the investor nets $60.40 after the .396 tax. After 10 years the investor will have $108.58.

$$60.40(1.0604)^{10} = \$108.58$$

If the firm retains \$100 for 10 years earning .10 per year and then the firm is sold, the investor nets

$$100(1.10)^{10}(1 - .20) = \$207.50$$

The advantage of retention is \$98.92, which is a .91 increase over \$108.50, the future amount with a dividend.

If the corporation retains, the investor gives up \$60.40 at time 0 and then nets \$207.50 after tax at time 10. This is an IRR of .131.

$$60.40(1 + IRR)^{10} = 207.50$$
$$IRR = .131$$

This IRR is smaller than with the shorter time horizon. But let us consider the present value. With a five-year horizon the present value of the \$47.86 advantage of retention is \$35.70.

$$PV = (1.0604)^{-5} \, 47.86 = \$35.70$$

With a 10-year horizon the present value of the \$98.22 advantage of retention is \$55.03:

$$PV = (1.0604)^{-10} \, 98.22 = \$55.03$$

The present value of the advantage of retention increases as the horizon is increased, but the IRR earned by the investor decreases if the corporation retains rather than pays a dividend and the horizon is increased.

Dividends of Many Periods

In the preceding example we consider only the dividend of one year. But assume a \$100 dividend for five years (first dividend is at time 0). The future value for five years is:

$$\text{Future value} = [100(1.0604)^5 + 100B(4, .0604)(1.0604)^5](1 - .396)$$

TABLE 4.1 Value at Time 5

Time			Value at Time 5
0	$100 (1.10)^5$	=	$161.05
1	$100 (1.10)^4$	=	146.41
2	$100 (1.10)^3$	=	133.10
3	$100 (1.10)^2$	=	121.00
4	$100 (1.10)^1$	=	110.00
	Value		$671.56

where $B(4, .0604)$ is the present value of an annuity with the first payment one year from now and equal to $\dfrac{1-(1.604)^{-4}}{.0604} = 3.4619$.

Future value = $[134.08 + 346.19(1.3408)].604 = \$361.33$

If the corporation retains \$100 a year for five years and earns .10 per year it will have \$671.56 at time 5 (see Table 4.1).
The investor will net after tax \$537.25:

$$(1 - .2)671.56 = \$537.25$$

The advantage of retention compared to dividends is now \$175.92 or an increase of

$$\frac{175.92}{361.33} = .49$$

CONCLUSIONS

Private equity is not likely to attract investors who want the corporation to pay cash dividends. The advantages of retention and then capital gains compared to immediate cash dividends are very large for investors paying a high tax rate.

Private equity allows a corporation to follow a 100 percent retention policy without harming those investors who want cash dividends. The cash dividend preferring investors should place their funds elsewhere. The strategy for firms with private equity capital is to avoid cash dividends and have the investors benefit from future capital gains.

A board of directors acting in the interests of the stockholders of a public corporation sets the dividend policy of a firm to please many different types of investors. The ability of an investor to defer income taxes as a result of the company's retaining earnings is an important consideration. In addition, the distinction between ordinary income and capital gains for purposes of income taxation by the federal government accentuates the importance of the investors knowing the dividend policy of the firms whose stock they are considering purchasing or have already purchased. Some investors face zero or low tax rates and have different objectives from the high tax rate investors. This means that a corporation (and its board) has a responsibility to announce its dividend policy, and attempt to be consistent in its policy, changing only when its economic situation changes significantly.

Private equity simplifies the task of a firm's board of directors since the equity investors are likely to have similar investment objectives. There is value added since the board of directors does not have to follow a distribution policy aimed at pleasing the average investor, given a narrow range of preferences among the private equity investors.

QUESTIONS AND PROBLEMS

1a. Assume an investor can earn .12 before investor tax and .07248 after investor tax. The tax rate on ordinary income is .396. If the corporation pays a $100 dividend, after 20 years the investor will have how much?

1b. If the corporation retains the $100 and earns .12 per year for 20 years, the investor will have how much? Assume a .20 capital gains tax rate.

2. What IRR does the investor earn with retention compared to an immediate cash dividend?

3a. What is the value of a firm paying $100 dividend taxed at .396, with zero growth and a .07248 discount rate?

3b. Assume the $100 per year is reinvested for 20 years and the basic firm value of $833.33 is present at time 20.

$$FV = 100B(20, .12)(1.12)^{20} = \quad \$7,205.24$$
$$\underline{+\ 833.33}$$

Firm's Value $8,038.57

The firm's value at time 20 is $8,038.57.

Assume the $7,205.24 is sold at time 20 (assume a zero tax basis).

Tax = .2(7,205.24) = $1,441.05.

What is the present value of this strategy?

CHAPTER 5

A Changed Capital Structure

A second way that finance strategy combined with private equity adds value is by substituting debt for equity. The CEO of the typical large public firm is well paid, independent of the firm's performance. The CEO's financial rewards are likely to go up if the firm does well, but there are not likely to be significant reductions in pay if the firm does not reach its operating targets. If the CEO does badly enough, there is the possibility that the board of directors will fire the CEO. The CEO does not want to increase the variance of the outcomes for the stockholders larger than necessary. Additions to debt in substitution for stock always increase the variance of the stockholders' returns. By keeping the amount of debt low, the CEO of a highly profitable firm is able to increase the likelihood of keeping a stream of high income. For most managers the present value of their salaries is larger than their value increment from substituting debt for equity.

Now consider private equity where management owns a significant percentage of the common stock. The objectives of gaining control and increasing firm value are now more competitive with the likelihood of the CEO's retaining the position and salary. The incentive to substitute debt for equity is larger than when the CEO was just an employee.

THE MOTIVATIONS FOR USING DEBT

There are many reasons why the use of debt might be desirable but we will concentrate on three. The first is that the nominal cost of debt is less than the current cost of equity; thus the expected return on equity can be increased by the use of debt. While this option is intuitively attractive, we cannot argue that the total firm value is increased for this reason.

The second reason for using debt is based on the tax law that allows debt interest to be tax deductions, but recognizes no tax deduction for the return on an equity security. We shall see that the tax deductibility of interest can add significantly to the value of a firm with the amount of value added depending on the corporate income before tax, the corporate tax rate, and the amount of new debt. The investor tax rates also affect the analysis.

The third reason is the most important for private equity. The debt facilitates accomplishing the acquisition of the firm. It helps get the deal done.

Debt Costs Less than Equity

Assume that debt costs .06 if .5 of the capital is debt and in one period a $1,000 investment has a .10 expected return. Note the investment has a higher return than the debt cost. There are zero taxes. The situation is as shown in Table 5.1.

With 100 percent equity, the stockholders earn .10. With 50 percent debt and 50 percent equity the stockholders can expect to earn .14. This is called "trading on the equity" and it is typical of one justification for using debt (the use of debt enhances the expected return on the stock).

An investor who buys both debt and equity (in equal amounts) will again earn the .10 unlevered return. Without taxes and with a rational capital market no value is added by substituting debt for equity. The investor can replicate the firm's use of

TABLE 5.1   Investment Has a Higher Return than Debt Cost

	0	1	Return and Costs
Investment	–1,000	+1,100	.10
Debt	+500	–530	.06
Common stock	+500	–570	.14

debt by borrowing and can delever the leveraged firm by buying both debt and equity.

The use of the debt results in a larger spread of outcomes for the stockholders. Assume the outcomes at time 1 for the $1,000 investment are as shown in Table 5.2.

With the set of possible outcomes the $500 of initial debt is always paid the contractual amount of $530. The stockholders face the outcomes shown in Table 5.3 (the equity investment is $500).

The spread of outcomes (IRR) on the common stock investment is much larger with the $500 of debt than it was with 100 percent of stock.

Assume that if $900 of debt is used, the debt cost will be increased to .07. See Table 5.4.

The expected return on the common stock is increased from .10 with no debt, to .14 with .5 debt, to .37 with .9 debt. But again there

TABLE 5.2 Investment Outcomes at Time 1

Event	Probability	Investment Outcome (Time 1)	IRR
e^1	.5	$1,670	.67
e^2	.5	530	−.47

TABLE 5.3 Outcomes for Stockholders

Event	Probability	Time 1 Stock Return	IRR
e^1	.5	$1,140	1.28
e^2	.5	0	−1.00

TABLE 5.4 $900 of Debt

	0	1	Return and Costs
Investment	−1,000	+1,100	.10
Debt	+ 900	− 963	.07
Common Stock	+ 100	− 137	.37

is no reason to conclude value has been added by the substitution of debt for equity. To add value for the stockholders, we must consider corporate taxes.

DEBT USE AND TAXES

The conventional valuation model with the firm issuing B of debt in substitution for stock equity assumes:

$$V_L = V_U + tB \qquad (5.1)$$

where V_L = the value of the leveraged firm
V_U = the value of the firm before debt is substituted for equity
t = the corporate tax rate
B = the amount of debt that is added

The assumptions are that the debt added in substitution for stock is outstanding for perpetuity and that there are no costs of financial distress. The term tB is equal to the present value of the tax savings from the debt interest deductions.

Example
Assume a firm earns $153.85 per year before corporate tax and $100 after corporate tax ($t = .35$). There is no growth and the stockholders use a .08 discount rate.

$$V_U = \frac{100}{.08} = \$1,250$$

The value of the unleveraged firm is $1,250.

Now assume that $1,000 of .06 debt is substituted for $1,000 of stock. The value of the leveraged firm (with no cost of financial distress) is

$$V_L = 1,250 + .35(1,000) = \$1,600$$

Since there is now $1,000 of debt and the value of the firm is $1,600 the new value of the stock is $600. The stockholders also receive the $1,000 of debt proceeds, thus have total wealth of $1,600 (they previously had an investment of $1,250). The $350 increase in stockholder wealth is equal to tB.

Without debt the investors earned $100 per year. With $1,000 of .06 debt we have

Debt	.06(1,000)	$ 60
Stock	(153.85 – 60)(1 – .35)	61
	Total	$121

After the debt issuance the debt and equity investors receive $121 in total.

Assume stockholders want to earn the same return as that earned by the stock if the firm were unleveraged, and to achieve this goal they buy .65 of the debt and 1.00 of the stock. The amount of debt being purchased is equal to $(1 - t)$ of the outstanding debt where t is the corporate tax rate. The investors following this strategy would earn

Debt .65(60)	$ 39
Stock	61
Total	$100

The returns from the stock of the unleveraged firm and the returns from the investment in the debt and stock of the leveraged firm are equal. In fact, with the given investment strategy, they are always equal for any value of EBIT.

Assume the common stock of the unleveraged firm earns X before tax and with a .35 corporate tax $(1 - t)X = .65X$ after tax. Buying .65 of the debt and 1.00 of the stock of the leveraged firm the investor earns

Debt	.65(60)	39
Stock	$(X - 60)(1 - t)$	$.65X - 39$
	Total	$.65X$

The two investment returns are equal for any value of X.

The strategy was to buy $(1 - t)$ or $.65$ of the debt. This investment strategy results in the investment in the leveraged firm being equal to the return in the unleveraged firm. Assuming the two investments have the same value (they have the same benefits), then

$$V_U = S + (1 - t)B$$

where S is the stock value of the leveraged firm. Since by definition $V_L = S + B$ then $V_L = V_U + tB$.

This relationship can be derived in several different ways. For example, there are interest expenses of kB if the debt interest rate is k. The tax saving is tkB with a present value (assuming the tax savings are a perpetuity and k is the discount rate) of tB:

$$PV = \frac{tkB}{k} = tB$$

which can be added to V_U to obtain V_L.

THE USE OF THE CASH

How do the stockholders benefit from the issuance of $1,000 of debt in substitution of debt for stock?

- The debt can be issued directly to the stockholders.
- The debt can be issued to the public and the $1,000 cash can be paid as a dividend to the firm's shareholders.
- The debt can be issued to the public for cash and the $1,000 cash can be used by the firm to repurchase stock (for most firms this is the best solution).
- The debt can be issued to the public for $1,000 cash and the $1,000 cash can be used by the firm to buy assets. This would require a slightly different model from the one illustrated in this chapter.

COSTS OF FINANCIAL DISTRESS

For some firms there are large costs of financial distress (both suppliers and customers disappear or one of the two disappears) and there are significant probabilities of these events occurring if debt is substituted for stock. The more debt outstanding the larger the likelihood of distress occurring. Thus with more debt the tax savings increase but so do the costs of financial distress. At how much debt do the incremental tax benefits from debt equal the change in financial distress costs of debt? For many firms the expected costs of financial distress are relatively small and these firms can use a large amount of debt compared to stock.

DEFINING THE DETERMINANTS OF CORPORATE BORROWING

Assume a situation where there are no financial distress costs. Given the tax savings of debt a firm will issue debt (rather than equity) to finance acceptable investments, if the goal is to maximize shareholder wealth, and if there are no investor taxes. The limits of corporate borrowing, given an objective of maximizing shareholder wealth, are determined by the firm's ability to use the tax savings, by the costs of financial distress, and by the willingness of financial markets to lend. Debt usage is restricted, in the presence of desirable investments and an objective of maximizing shareholder wealth, only if there are costs of financial distress or investor taxes.

Without costs of financial distress, with a goal of maximizing shareholder wealth, the utilization of debt to finance desirable investments would be limited by the willingness of investors to lend and investor taxes, not by the willingness of the firm to borrow.

REASONS FOR USING DEBT

There are many valid reasons for corporations to use debt. Among the primary reasons are:

- Tax deductibility of interest (debt is cheaper than equity; thus debt increases the firm's value and reduces its cost of capital).
- Raise capital from banks quickly.
- Raising equity capital signals overvaluation so the firm issues debt, which signals optimism.
- Easier to increase ROE (if investment earns more than the cost of debt). Also may have a desirable effect on EPS.
- No dilution of voting control.
- Incentive to management and a constraint of management.
- Timing (common stock is depressed and capital is needed).
- Reduces the need for equity capital (using other people's money).
- A large amount of debt tends to discourage raiders.
- Debt has lower issue costs than new equity.

If management wants to maximize shareholder value, it will tend to use some debt in the firm's capital structure. The objective of the next sections of the chapter is to define the factors that limit the amount of debt issued by a firm, if the primary motivation for debt issuance is the income tax consideration and the primary goal is to maximize shareholder value.

TAX CONSIDERATIONS

The substitution of debt for equity reduces the firm's cost of capital (assuming zero costs of financial distress) and increases the firm's value. It can be readily shown that with zero investor taxes, zero agency costs, and zero costs of financial distress that

$$k_0 = k_e(0)\left(1 - t\frac{B}{V_L}\right) \tag{5.2}$$

and

$$V_L = V_U + tB \tag{5.1}$$

where k_0 = the weighted average cost of capital of a levered
                firm
$k_e(0)$ = the cost of equity capital of an unlevered firm
       t = the corporate tax rate
      B = the amount of debt to be issued in substitution for
                equity
      V_L = the value of the leveraged firm
      V_U = the value of the unleveraged firm

Assume the cost of capital with zero debt $[k_e(0)]$ is .15 and that debt is substituted for stock so that $\dfrac{B}{V_L}$ = .5. If the corporate tax rate is .35 then the cost of capital is reduced from .15 to .12375.

$$k_0 = .15[1 - .35(.5)] = .12375 \qquad (5.2)$$

If the value of the unleveraged firm (V_U) is $16,500,000 and $10,000,000 of debt ($B$) is substituted for stock then the value of the leveraged firm (V_L) is $20,000,000:

$$V_L = 16,500,000 + .35(10,000,000) = 20,000,000$$

and

$$\frac{B}{V_L} = \frac{1}{2} \qquad (5.1)$$

The conclusion based on these two formulations is to issue a maximum amount of debt. A maximum debt will increase the firm's value (V_L) and will reduce the firm's weighted average cost of capital (k_o) compared to using less than maximum debt. But a review of publicly traded firms reveals that few firms issue an amount of debt that is equal to the theoretical maximum (to be defined). The next section considers the factors that effectively limit the amount of debt a firm will want to issue in substitution for equity.

LIMITING THE USE OF DEBT

The list of factors limiting the amount of debt issued by a corporation in substitution of equity is long. It includes:

- The probability of timely utilization of tax savings from the debt interest is less than one, reducing the incremental expected value from substituting $1 of debt for equity as additional debt is issued.
- The expected costs of financial distress and bankruptcy. Adding debt increases the incremental risk to shareholders.
- The owners and/or managers fear loss of control because of the risk of bankruptcy. Bankruptcy might prevent the firm from reaching a pot of gold.
- The structure of investor taxes favor some equity.
- Debt indenture provisions limit managerial actions. Incremental debt limits the managerial and financial flexibility (the ability to take advantage of opportunities).
- An increase in debt leverage increases incremental cost of borrowing.
- The debt increases the firm's Beta and the variance of EPS and ROE. Management worries about the effects of too much debt on the stock price if the firm's leverage greatly exceeds that of comparable firms. It is feared that the stock market will interpret the substitution of debt for equity negatively.
- The changing of the capital structure may result in taxation of the equity investors accepting the debt in substitution for their equity securities.
- Cash flows out of the firm paying the debt interest will restrict growth of the firm.
- The economic characteristics of the firm's assets limit the amount of debt that can be supported.

All the above factors are relevant. Not all decision makers will be concerned with a negative reaction by the market, but for some managers the market reaction is the primary consideration. But usually management's objectives are more complex than the maximization of shareholder value.

Next, we consider how the economic characteristics of the firm's assets limit the amount of debt (issued in substitution for stock) that can be supported. If debt were being issued to acquire new assets the analysis would be different.

HOW THE FIRM'S ASSETS DETERMINE THE MAXIMUM DEBT

Assume equation (5.1) applies:

$$V_L = V_U + tB \qquad (5.1)$$

With maximum debt, $V_L = B$ and therefore:

$$B = V_U + tB$$

and solving for B:

$$B = \frac{V_U}{1-t} \qquad (5.3)$$

For the example where $V_U = \$16,500,000$ and $t = .35$, the value of B is:

$$B = \frac{16,500,000}{1-.35} = \$25,385,000 \qquad (5.3)$$

If more than \$25,385,000 of debt is issued in substitution for stock there is a significant likelihood that the firm would not be able to pay the contractual debt payments. This conclusion is based on the market's valuation of the unleveraged firm, thus includes the market's risk perceptions.

Let X be the firm's expected earnings before interest and taxes and equal to \$3,807,750. The maximum debt can also be determined using the earnings expected to be generated by the assets. If the expected earnings before taxes (the taxable income) X is a perpetuity, we have for the value of the unleveraged firm:

$$V_U = \frac{X(1-t)}{k_e(0)} \tag{5.4}$$

Substituting in (5.3) for V_U:

$$B = \frac{X}{k_e(0)} \tag{5.5}$$

where B is the maximum debt that can be issued if V_U is valid.

For the example where $X = \$3,807,750$ and $k_e(0) = .15$ consistent with the values of equation (5.3) and the assumption that $V_U = \$16,500,000$:

$$B = \frac{3,807,750}{.15} = \$25,385,000 \tag{5.5}$$

and

$$V_U = \frac{X(1-t)}{k_e(0)} = \frac{3,807,750(.65)}{.15} = \$16,500,000 \tag{5.4}$$

We also want the interest expense to be equal to or less than the expected taxable income assumed to be equal to X. If the debt has an interest cost of k_i then to be able to use effectively the interest tax deductions, it is necessary that:

$$k_i B \leq X$$

or

$$B \leq \frac{X}{k_i} \tag{5.6}$$

For the example, if $k_i = .15$ for the maximum debt, we have

$$B \leq \frac{3,807,750}{.15} = \$25,385,000 \qquad (5.6)$$

The maximum debt has already been computed to be $25,385,000 based on the firm's assets and the market's valuation of the assets. The ability of the firm to use the tax deductions is also an effective restraint. The cost of debt would have to equal or be larger than $k_e(0)$ for this constraint to be binding. A value of k_i equal to $k_e(0)$ is reasonable, given the fact that we are determining the maximum amount of debt that can be issued; thus the risk of the maximum debt is equal to the risk of the stock with zero debt.

The maximum amount of debt a firm can issue to this point has been determined by the firm's ability to earn income X, the firm's underlying required return $k_e(0)$, the amount of taxable income X, and the cost of debt, k_i. But the costs of financial distress must also be considered.

COSTS OF FINANCIAL DISTRESS: A MARGINAL ANALYSIS

Both the expected value of the tax savings and the expected costs of financial distress fit nicely conceptually into a marginal analysis. Managers should compare the expected incremental tax saving value increase from substituting debt for equity and the increase in the expected present value of the costs of financial distress. The costs of financial distress include the effects of financial distress on operations as well as the explicit legal costs of bankruptcy.

Assume $t = .35$, and the present value of the costs of financial distress is $30,000,000. For debt of $11,000,000 and $10,000,000 if there is probability one of the tax savings and the costs of financial distress being realized we have Table 5.5.

The use of $11,000,000 of debt is better than $10,000,000 with the given assumptions since the tax savings are larger. But the above analysis must be modified if the probabilities of being able to use the tax deductions (thus realize the tax savings) and the probabilities of incurring financial distress are not one. See Table 5.6.

TABLE 5.5 Probability One of the Tax Savings and the Costs of Financial Distress Being Realized

	Relevant Outcomes	
	Present Value of Tax Saving	Present Value of the Costs of Financial Distress
B $11,000,000	$3,850,000	$30,000,000
B $10,000,000	3,500,000	30,000,000
Incremental change	$ 350,000	$ 0

TABLE 5.6 If Probabilities Are Not One

	Relevant Probability Factors	
	Probability of Realizing Full Tax Saving	Probability of Costs of Financial Distress
B $11,000,000	.95	.11
B $10,000,000	1.00	.10

Multiplying the probability factors by the dollar outcomes and assuming either all or none of the tax savings can be used we have Table 5.7.

With these facts, despite the increase in the expected tax saving, the issuance of the extra $1,000,000 of debt is not desirable, given the $300,000 increase in the expected costs of financial distress.

Assume the probability of financial distress remains constant at

TABLE 5.7 Multiplying the Probability Factors by the Dollar Outcomes

	Expected Present Value of Tax Saving	Expected Present Value of Costs of Financial Distress
B $11,000,000	$3,657,500	$3,300,000
B $10,000,000	3,500,000	3,000,000
Expected incremental change	$ 157,500	$ 300,000

.10 as debt is increased from $10,000,000 to $11,000,000. Despite the fact that the probability of using the interest tax shield is reduced from one to .95, there is still $157,500 of expected value added by an additional $1,000,000 of debt for equity, even after $10,000,000 of debt has been issued. The probability of losing some of the value of the corporate tax shield from interest goes from zero to .05 but the incremental debt issuance is still desirable.

If we change the probability of financial distress with $10,000,000 of debt to zero and with $11,000,000 of debt to .001 so that the expected cost of financial distress with $11,000,000 of debt is $3,300, the issuance of the additional debt is desirable, given the expected increase in tax savings is $157,500.

To determine the desirability of substituting debt for equity, management must determine the expected value of incremental interest tax savings and compare this expectation with the value of the increase in the expected cost of financial distress. These expectations will depend on the firm, the industry, and the state of the economy. They are highly subjective; thus we can expect there to be differences of opinion as to the optimum amount of debt leverage if the interest tax savings and the costs of financial distress are not certain.

THE PREFERENCES OF MANAGEMENT

When a corporation encounters financial difficulty, it is likely to resort to debt financing to keep afloat. In this situation the firm can easily reach its debt capacity (to raise capital it has to pay a large interest rate, but the large rate tends to insure that it cannot pay the debt owed). But with a growing profitable firm the amount of debt used is likely to be well below the maximum debt amounts illustrated in the preceding example. Why does management stop well short of the debt amounts indicated by the models?

We have assumed to this point that the goal of the debt decision is to maximize the shareholders' value. But realistically, we cannot expect management and the board of directors to ignore the effect of the debt decision on their own well-being.

Consider a Chair of the Board who is receiving an annual wage (all elements considered) of $20,000,000. The Chair has an investment of $50,000,000 in the firm's common stock. If the firm uses maximum debt the value of this stock is expected to increase to $76,923,000, an increase of $26,923,000, but the probability of financial distress in the next three years goes from .01 to .99. With financial distress the Chair loses the job. From the viewpoint of the Chair, is the debt issuance desirable? Not only is the Chair placing the $20,000,000 per year and the common stock investment in jeopardy, but also the Chair loves the job. With these facts the Chair will drastically scale back the amount of debt to be issued. The management's performance is measured by the bottom line (earnings to shareholders), and the presence of a large amount of debt with a fixed interest expense increases the likelihood that the year's income will be negative. A loss incurred by the firm increases the probability that the top management will be replaced.

Secondly, debt may limit managerial actions. The debt indenture frequently restricts the actions management can take under certain conditions. For example, the ability to issue more debt to exploit desirable investment opportunities is reduced and any incremental debt issued will be at a higher cost since there is already a large amount of debt outstanding.

Third, the senior managers of a corporation have legitimate concerns regarding the effect of the issuance of debt in substitution for equity on the stock price. The stock market might interpret the effect of substitution of debt for equity negatively and shareholder value may be adversely affected. Conventional wisdom is that a firm's capital structure should be similar to that of other firms in its industry and the market will penalize departures from the norm. Also important is the fact that even if there were to be a positive effect on shareholder value, the value increase might not be perceived as exceeding the cost incurred by the managers in terms of the loss of job security.

These views of top management are a major hurdle preventing the implementation of an aggressive capital structure.

THE COSTS OF CHANGING CAPITAL STRUCTURE

There are transaction and tax costs of changing a capital structure. The transaction costs of an exchange offer are relatively low, so we do not expand on that aspect. The tax considerations for the investors, however, can be material. Assume the substitution of debt for equity results in a taxable transaction that is either ordinary income (a dividend) or a capital gain (a share repurchase).

First, assume a situation where the current stock price is less than the tax basis of the common stock so that the value of the debt received on the exchange will be less than the tax basis. The investor who exchanges will have a tax loss and the exchange may have beneficial tax consequences to this investor.

However, if the current stock price exceeds the tax basis, there will be a tax created by the exchange. There are several possibilities:

- The investor is a tax-exempt entity, thus no tax is created.
- The investor is a corporation that would prefer a dividend and the 70 percent dividend received deduction.
- The investor is an individual taxed at .20 on capital gains (thus prefers a share repurchase) and .396 on ordinary income (thus would prefer to avoid a dividend).

Given the different tax situations that exist with a normal mix of investors, the only conclusion that we can reach is that there can be significant tax consequences to the investors that should be considered as debt is substituted for equity.

THE TAX ADVANTAGE OF EQUITY

Normally, debt has a tax advantage over equity because of the tax deductibility of interest, but this is not always the situation. Assume a group of investors who pay .396 tax on ordinary income and .20 on capital gains. An equity investment combined with retention might be more desirable than debt, even though the debt interest offers a tax shield at the corporate level.

Assume a firm earns $100 before tax and with a .35 corporate tax rate, $65 after tax. If the $65 is reinvested by the corporation to earn .10 for 20 years and the accumulation is then taxed to stockholders at .20, the investors net

$$65(1.10)^{20}(1 - .20) = \$350$$

If the $100 earned by the corporation is paid to the investors as interest the investor nets $60.40 after a .396 tax. Invested in debt to earn .0604 per year in the same corporation for 20 years, the investor nets: $60.40(1.0604)^{20} = \$195.18$. Common stock is significantly more desirable (assuming equivalent risk).

CONCLUSIONS

The maximum value of a firm with an initial value of V_U as a result of substituting debt for equity is $V_L = \dfrac{V_U}{1-t}$. With $t = .35$ we have $V_L = 1.538V_U$. The firm's unlevered value can be increased by .538, at the most, by the use of debt. This amount of increase from issuing debt changes if the tax rate changes or if we consider the costs of financial distress or the taxation of investors.

It is reasonable (given human nature) for a publicly owned corporation to use less than an optimum amount of debt. With a firm financed with private equity it is reasonable to expect a larger degree of debt utilization.

QUESTIONS AND PROBLEMS

1. Assume a $800 investment returns $1,000 at time 1 (a .25 return). What is the IRR on $100 of equity if $700 of .08 debt is used as well as equity?

2a. Assume the value of a firm's equity is $1,000 and $800 of .10 debt is substituted for equity. The corporate tax rate is .35.

    What is the new value of the equity?

    What total wealth do the stockholders have?

2b. If the debt rate is used as the discount rate, what is the present value of the interest tax savings?

3a. Assume a firm with a value of $10,000 earns $1,000 EBIT. The tax rate is .35. An investor owning 100 percent of the equity earns how much?

3b. If the firm earning $1,000 EBIT is financed with .90 debt ($9,000) that pays .08 and .10 equity, the investor (who owns 100% of the equity) buys .65 of the debt. What return (in dollars) does the investor earn?

3c. Compare your answers to (3a.) and (3b.). What do you observe?

3d. Recompute your answers to (3a.) and (3b.) if the firm earns $2,000 EBIT.

4. Change the cost of debt of problem 3b. to .10. Recompute the investor's return if the firm earns $2,000 EBIT.

5. A firm with a value of $1,000 and zero debt has a cost of capital of .12. Assume $900 of .08 debt is substituted for stock. The tax rate is .35. Estimate the new cost of capital.

6. Assume the value of an unlevered firm is $10,000,000. The tax rate is .35.

    What is the maximum amount of debt that can be issued in substitution for equity if the $10,000,000 is an accurate measure?

    How much value can be added?

7a. Assume a one year investment of $10,000 returns $10,900 at time 1. What is the return on $1,000 of equity if $9,000 of .05 debt is used? Assume zero taxes.

7b. What is the IRR (after tax) on $1,000 of equity if the firm earns $12,000 before tax? The tax rate is .35.

    With no debt, what is the IRR on equity?

8a. The market capitalization of a firm with 100 percent stock equity is $10,000,000. Assume $8,000,000 of .10 debt is substituted for stock (the debt is given to the shareholders). The tax rate is .35. There are no costs of financial distress. What is the value of the firm after the debt is issued? What is the value of the stock?

8b. If the stockholders had no other assets, how much wealth would they have after the debt is issued?

8c. If the interest rate on the debt was .05 rather than .10, how do your answers to questions 2b. and 3a. change?

8d. If the firm's weighted average cost of capital were .15 with zero debt, what would it be with $8,000,000 of .10 debt?

8e. How low can one reduce the WACC by changing the capital structure?

CHAPTER 6

Merchant Banking

Merchant banking is the very old art of a banking firm's collecting funds from investors (who have sufficient wealth to qualify as investors) to invest in enterprises. In recent years the term has been applied to firms that engage in private equity types of activity. In this chapter we consider the finance related value added by merchant banking activity. The equity component of the operating firm is private equity capital.

NO STOCK PRICE CHANGE

Appendix 1 shows that with the assumptions that the ending stock price is equal to the beginning stock price (no growth by the firm) and that dividends are constant the length of the time horizon is not relevant and the value is

$$P_o = \frac{(1 - t_p)D}{r_p}$$

where P_o = the initial stock price
D = the dividend (constant)
t_p = the investor's tax rate on ordinary income
r_p = the investor's after tax opportunity cost on comparable risk equity investments
n = the horizon in years

The numbers in the following examples are rounded off.

Example

Let $t_p = .396$, $r_p = .07248$, $D = \$100$, $t_g = .20$

$$P_o = \frac{(1-t_p)D}{r_p} = \frac{60.40}{.07248} = \$833$$

P_o is independent of n. By assuming no stock price change, effectively, we have assumed the dividend stream is a perpetuity. Investors buying the stock at a price of \$833 earn .07248. For the buyer to break even (earn a return of .07248), a price of \$833 can be offered for the stock of the firm.

If dividends grow at a rate of g then it is necessary to compute the present value of the growing dividend. The following modified formula would be used if r_p is larger than g and if g continues for perpetuity:

$$P_o = \frac{(1-t_p)D}{r_p - g}$$

The Terminal Value Is Zero

Now assume the stock price at time n is zero. The investors will have a tax loss of P_o with a tax saving of $t_g P_o$ where t_g is the assumed tax rate on capital losses. Continuing the example with $t_g = .2$ and $n = 5$ we have:

$$P_o = (1 - t_p)D \times B(n,r_p) + t_g P_o(1 + r_p)^{-n}$$
$$P_o = 246.02 + .2P_o(.7048)$$
$$.859P_o = 246.02$$
$$P_o = \$286$$

where $B(n, r_p) = \dfrac{1-(1+r_p)^{-n}}{r_p}$ is the present value of an annuity for n years using r_p as the discount rate. The term $t_g P_o(1 + r_p)^{-n}$ is the present value of the tax savings $(t_g P_o)$ from a P_o capital loss taken at time n, if the investor has a time value opportunity cost of r_p. The changed assumption from an infinite life to a five year life with a zero value at time 5 reduced the stock value from $833 to $286.

Retention and Then Capital Gain

Assume the firm retains earnings for n time periods earning r each year and then this accumulation is distributed and taxed at a t_g rate. The initial tax basis is $833.

$$r = .12, r_p = .07248, \text{ and } n = 5$$

In addition to the value of retention and then distribution assume there is basic firm value of $833 at time 5 (see preceding calculations). The value of the stock at time 0 is $945.50.

$$P_o = (1 + r_p)^{-n}[(1 - t_g)(RE)B(n,r)(1 + r)^n + 833]$$
$$P_o = 358 + 587 = \$945$$

The term $(RE)B(n,r)(1 + r)^n$ is the future value (at time n) of RE per year retained to earn

$$r = .12 \text{ per year}$$

The firm earning .12 with retained earnings when $r_p = .072848$ adds value. The stock value is now $945 because of the retained earnings for five years rather than annual dividends. The present value added by retention for five years is $945 − 833 = $112.

THE INVESTOR'S IRR

Assume the cost of buying a firm paying a constant perpetual $100 dividend is $833 (this is the tax basis). The investor can earn .07248 in the market. After purchase, assume five years of retention with the firm earning .12 and then a capital gain. The firm has other value of $833 at time 5. This is based on the market assuming future annual dividends of $100 beginning at time 6 and no earnings retention after five years.

Let j be the investor's IRR for the five year investment.

$$833 = (1 + j)^{-5}[(1 - .20)100B(5, .12)(1.12)^5 + 833]$$
$$(1 + j)^5 = 1.60988$$
$$j = .100$$

The investor earns .100 after tax, if the firm follows the described strategy. With the first example, the investor earned only .07248 from the dividend paying firm that was selling for $833.

Substituting Debt

Now assume $800 of .08 zero coupon debt with a life of five years is used to finance $800 of the initial $833 purchase price. The equity component of the investment is $33. The corporate tax rate is .35.

Future value of debt = $800(1.08)^5 = \$1,175$ (See Table 6.1.)

The corporation has basic after tax cash flows of $100 per year for five years and is able to reinvest to earn a .12 return. The future value of the $100 retained cash flows per year is $635.

$$FV = 100B(5, .12)(1.12)^5 = \$635$$

TABLE 6.1 Interest Tax Savings

Time	Debt	Interest (.08)	Tax Saving	Period
0	800	64	22	1
1	864	69	24	2
2	933	75	26	3
3	1,008	81	28	4
4	1,088	87	30	5
5	1,175			
			$FV(.12) = \$182$	

TABLE 6.2   Equity Value

Total firm value at time 5 = 635 + 833 + 182	$1,650
Debt payment = $800(1.08)^5$	−1,175
Value of stock equity	475
Tax basis of stock	33
Taxable gain of shareholders	$ 442
Tax rate	.2
Investor's tax	$ 88

If the debtholders are not taxed, they net $1,175 at time 5. The tax savings on the debt interest, reinvested by the corporation to earn .12, will have a future value of $182.

Assume the stock after the payment of the debt at time 5 will have a remaining value of $475. The total firm value at time 5 is $1,650 before the debt payment of $1,175.

The investor's value is $387 (net of $88 tax) (see Table 6.2).

The equity investors net $387:

$$475 - 88 = \$387$$

The stockholders invested $33 and five years later they net $387 (after tax) and earn an annual IRR of .63.

$$33(1 + j)^5 = 387$$
$$j = .636$$

The small ($33) equity investment enables the equity investors to earn the .636 annual return even though the corporation earns only .12 on new investments.

FACTORS CONTRIBUTING TO INCREMENTAL VALUE

There are four factors contributing to the incremental value and large IRR earned by the stockholders.

1. Capital gain rate (.2) applied to the gain instead of ordinary income rate (.396)
2. Investor tax deferral (tax at time 5 rather than each year)
3. Debt tax shield (interest)
4. Firm earns more (.12) after tax than debt costs (.052) after tax

The calculations that follow show that investors as a group earn .134. This is more than the .10 equity holders earned with the firm financed entirely by stock, because of the tax effects from using debt, and assuming that investors who buy the debt do not pay taxes.

Total Return
Assume investors net after tax (at time 5):

Debt	$1,175
Equity	387
Total	$1,562

With an initial $833 investment the IRR of the investors as a group is .134:

$$833(1 + j)^5 = 1,562$$
$$j = .134 \text{ (up from .07248 or .100)}$$

Debt earns .08 and equity earns .636. The $833 investment earns .134. The .08 return on the debt assumes the debt buyers do not pay any taxes. The zero tax investors buy the debt and the high tax $(t_g = .20)$ investors buy the stock.

An Extension: Changing the Horizon

Assume that investors can, at a cost of $833, earn cash flows of $1,562 five years later.

$$833(1 + j)^5 = \$1,562$$
$$j = .134 = IRR$$

Assume an alternative is to invest $833 (same cost as the preceding project) for 10 years and earn $2,587 and earn an IRR of .12:

$$833(1 + r)^{10} = \$2,587$$
$$r = .12$$

Which alternative is better for the investors?

Assume the investors' opportunity cost for capital is .07248 if the funds are invested in the market. Note that the horizon for the second alternative is 10 years.

If starting at the end of year 5 the investors with $1,562 can earn .106 (after tax), they will again have $2,587 at time 10.

$$1,562(1 + r)^5 = \$2,587$$
$$j = .106$$

Invest for 10 years at a return of .12 and earn .106 for the years 6 to 10.

This is acceptable given $r_p = .07248$.

If the investors can beat .106 (after tax) for years 6 to 10 by investing in the market, the first alternative is more desirable than the alternative of earning .12 over 10 years. Of course, uncertainty and risk preferences would affect the choice.

A Long Horizon

The dividend paying firm's value in the preceding example is computed to be $833 when the terminal value is $833 and this value is independent of the period of time that is assumed. But as an alternative assume the firm's value of $833 grows by .12 for 30 years and then a capital gain is realized.

$$833(1.12)^{30} = \$24,957$$

The firm's value at the end of 30 years is $24,957. With a tax rate of .20 and a $833 tax basis the investor's tax on sale at time 30 is $4,825.

$$.20(24,957 - 833) = \$4,825$$

and the investor nets

$$24,957 - 4,825 = \$20,132$$

The present value of the $20,132 net amount is

$$PV = 20,132(1.07248)^{-30} = \$2,467$$

The present value of the equity is increased from $833 (with an annual dividend of $100) to $2,467 (with retention for 30 years and a growth rate of .12 per year).

Now assume an infinite lived debt of $1,000 is issued at time 0 and that the debt adds $tB = .35(1,000) = \$350$ of value. The new firm value is 2,467 + 350 = $2,817. If the firm is purchased for $833 the net gain from retaining earnings rather than a dividend and the substitution of $1,000 of debt for stock results in a net gain (on a present value basis) of

$$2,817 - 833 = \$1,984$$

The $833 investment has turned into a value of $2,817 for the firm. Even more impressively the issue of $1,000 debt results in a net cash flow of $167 at time 0, given the $833 investment cost and an equity value net of debt of $1,817.

$$2,817 - 1,000 = \$1,817$$

THE PAYMENTS TO THE ORIGINATING FUND

Why do LBO management firms such as KKR play in the LBO game? Of course, they hope to earn a high return on their equity investment. But equally important they are paid 1 percent to 2 percent of the LBO's total assets each year as well as 15 percent to 25 percent of the profits. These payments to the managing firm are normally before any payments to the other investors, but there are exceptions where the other investors get the equivalent to a risk free return (approximately) before the payments to the LBO management firm.

CONCLUSIONS

- ■ The expected IRR for merchant banking increases if more debt is used and the cost of the debt is less than the firm's expected return.
- ■ The investment horizon affects the expected IRR earned on equity.
- ■ There may be zero tax for capital gains if the gains are not realized.
- ■ No operational advantages are assumed, but they are very important and can greatly affect the terminal value.

This chapter has focused attention on the gains from converting a cash dividend into retention and capital gains, and substituting debt for equity. But there are other gains from the use of private equity capital that must be considered. These are discussed in Chapters 7 and 8.

APPENDIX 1

We want to show that with the ending stock price equal to the beginning stock price the time horizon is not relevant.

Let P_o be the initial stock price. Then if the stock is worth P_o at time n:

$$P_o = (1 - t_p)D \times B(n, r_p) + P_o(1 + r_p)^{-n}$$

By definition

$$B(n, r_p) = \frac{1 - (1 + r_p)^{-n}}{r_p}$$

and

$$P_o[1-(1+r_p)^{-n}] = \frac{(1-t_p)D}{r_p}[1-(1+r_p)^{-n}]$$

Solving for P_o

$$P_o = \frac{(1-t_p)D}{r_p}$$

The terms containing the n value all drop out.

QUESTIONS AND PROBLEMS

1a. A firm is paying $8 per year dividend (the next dividend is in one year). There is zero growth. The tax rate on ordinary income is .396. The investor's after tax opportunity cost on comparable risk investments is .12.

What is the stock price?

1b. What is the stock price if the horizon being considered is five years and the stock price at time 5 is the same as at time zero?

1c. Assume a 20 year horizon. At the end of 20 years the stock value is expected to be zero. The capital gains tax rate is .20.

2. A firm is earning $8 per year. It can earn .20 (after corporate tax) on reinvested funds. Based on a constant dividend the firm's value is $40.27. If the funds are reinvested the firm's value after five years is estimated at

$$P_5 = (1.20)^5 40.27 = \$100.20$$

The investor has a .20 capital gains tax rate and a .07248 after tax opportunity cost for capital.

What is the value of this stock if the tax basis is $40.27? Assume the investor sells at time 5.

CHAPTER 7

Operations: The Other Factor

T he previous chapters have shown that value can be more than doubled by changing the firm's dividend policy, and a capital structure change (substituting debt for equity) can increase the stockholder's value by more than 50 percent. But if the firm is earning $1 these financial strategies will add little absolute dollar value. For the financial strategies to be significant there have to be profitable operations.

WHY CAN PRIVATE EQUITY RESULT IN ENHANCED PROFITABILITY?

Fewer Distractions

The need for publicly traded firms to meet short-term income goals is well known. Security analysts forecast a firm's next quarter's income per share and then the firm has to beat that forecast. Just meeting the forecast is not adequate since it shows an inability of the firm to beat the forecast. Do not blame the current author. He is only the messenger.

Why do firms become slaves to the notion that they must meet or beat an expected earnings per share number set by one or more security analysts? A few firms have said to analysts, "We will not help you estimate the next quarter's earnings and we will make no effort to meet or beat your estimate." Most firms rather help the analysts make sensible forecasts, but too often the analysts come up with estimates that cannot possibly be reached.

A private equity firm does not have analysts. Any earnings targets are set by the management and owners for their own use. A failure to meet a target is not the subject of headlines and wild stock price fluctuations.

Two Functions: One Person

The most popular form of a private equity firm is where management is a material part of the buyout group. We could call this a managerial buyout (MBO) but for simplicity we will use the term *private equity firm* to describe all buyouts.

With a publicly held firm management generally owns a small percentage of the equity, thus tends to make decisions from the viewpoint of management (their own self-interest) rather than the viewpoint of the shareholders. The fact that many managers act completely in the interests of the shareholders does not alter the conclusion that there are others who put their own interests first.

With a private equity firm where management owns a significant percentage of the equity, the interests of management and the owners are better aligned. Management has an incentive to make decisions that are more consistent with the shareholders' interests.

Nose to Grindstone

Frequently with a private equity firm management is encouraged to invest more than they can comfortably afford. The result is that management has an added incentive for the firm to do well. While it is reasonable to assume that management tried to have the firm do well before the firm went private, it is also reasonable to conclude that they will try harder when a large percentage of their wealth is invested in the firm's private equity.

Streamlined Decision Making

The management of a division of a multidivision corporation has many layers of the firm's management to convince before they can take important actions. Investment decisions have the potential to be particularly frustrating since frequently capital is not allocated among divisions in a manner that is consistent with the division's cash flow generation. A division might generate $100,000,000 of cash flow but only be allowed to invest $5,000,000. While the allocation might seem to be wise from the viewpoint of the corporate strategy, it can be frustrating for the division managers who see profitable investment opportunities slipping from their grasps. It is particularly annoying when an investment is approved but not in a timely fashion with the result that the realized income is much less than the original forecasted income because of the bad timing.

Impatience with Fools

A large corporation will too often be patient with managers who act in a foolish manner. There was one manager of a struggling division who loved automobile racing and spent outrageous sums financing cars and drivers as well as holding large expensive parties at the races. When the division became a stand-alone firm, the equity owner–managers immediately stopped this drainage of resources. Action is likely to be taken more rapidly with a private equity firm.

I suggest you play a game. At what hotel do you stay and where do you eat when you have to go to your favorite city on business? Do the answers change when you are paying the bill? What class do you fly on business? What class do you fly on vacation? Most people have different spending habits on expense accounts than when it is their own money. This is human nature, not good and evil. As soon as it is the managers' own money, spending habits change.

The fact that many managers of publicly held firms act as if corporate spending were out of their own pockets does not change the conclusion. Private equity capital firms are likely to spend the funds more efficiently than the managers of publicly owned firms.

Since the private equity firm is likely to be short of cash in the early years, the conservation of cash is frequently a necessity rather than the result of an arbitrary decision. In the early years more LBO firms are cash constrained and efficient cash flow management becomes a major management objective.

Roll-ups

In a roll-up private equity organizes a corporation that then acquires a series of small retail operations such as funeral parlors, printing shops, and so on. The objective is to introduce a brand name and efficiencies.

Unfortunately, the dedication of the owner–manager is frequently lost with the result that roll-ups have not always been successes.

Consolidations

With a consolidation the private equity lead manager convinces five to ten owner–managers that they would benefit from being part of a much larger corporation. The firms being consolidated are in different aspects of the same industry.

The consolidation offers the prospect of marketing and production efficiencies as well as better planned research and development. Frequently the small corporations are lacking in one or another type of managerial skill.

A by-product effect is that the larger corporation tends to attract a larger P/E in the stock market.

Some consolidations have been significant financial successes with the result that both the private equity and the component corporations have done very well.

CONCLUSIONS

Since many managers would act identically with a publicly held firm and a private equity firm, it is difficult for these managers to understand the issues discussed in this chapter. I concede that these managers do exist. But even with these managers, the management control system of a publicly held firm might prevent them from performing at maximum efficiency.

However, there are also many managers who will perform differently when they own a significant percentage of the firm's stock. These managers need to have their interests as management and their interests as owners better aligned. The private equity format (an LBO or MBO or something else) is a way of achieving that objective.

A successful private equity firm will tend to be the result of a highly successful operations modification as well as an intelligent financial strategy. The need to manage a private equity firm aggressively is large and the firm's success will hinge on operations. It is very rare to have a pure financial success with a private equity firm. More likely the success is based on improved and profitable operations.

CHAPTER 8

The Many Virtues of Going Public

This book is about private equity capital and its advantages, both financial and operational. But in the real world most corporations are publicly owned. Why do we observe omnipresent publicly owned corporations? Also, most private equity capital firms are en route to becoming publicly owned.

LIQUIDITY

Probably the number one reason for preferring an investment in publicly held firms compared to private equity firms is the liquidity of the equity investment. The holders of private equity tend to have a problem when they go to sell their common stock. Finding a buyer is difficult since there is no ready market for private equity. Also, the investor may be precluded by contract from selling the stock to the highest bidder.

The lack of liquidity is particularly apparent when the investor dies and the heirs have to pay inheritance taxes. If stock is sold to satisfy taxes or to achieve diversification, there is very likely to be a difference of opinion as to the price at which the transaction should take place.

PRICE

The price at which the investor is willing to sell the private equity stock depends on liquidity preferences. Without a market price the definitions of terms and a formula for computing the exit price become important. It is much more satisfying to sell at a market price than it is to have someone set an artificial price without reference to a market price. The seller will tend to think the price being set is too low and the buyers will think the price is too high. An impersonal market price is a tremendous improvement compared to the setting of a subjective price that is likely not to please anyone.

Also, the time that is allowed to pass before an offer is accepted affects the price that will be achieved. Too short a time period allowed for the sale to take place will reduce the expected price for the shares.

THE MARKET IS IMPERSONAL

The capital market is impersonal and one only has oneself to blame if the stock sale takes place at the wrong price. With private equity transactions it is easy to be resentful of a friend selling you stock that is now worth less than the price at which the stock was purchased. The transaction is no longer impersonal. Publicly traded stock offers many advantages when it is time for private equity holders to sell the stock.

FAMILY COMPLEXITIES

A private equity firm family business can run very smoothly as long as the founders are young and healthy enough to be effective. But complexities arise when the second, third, and fourth generations start receiving the shares and exercising control. At best, the family arrangement becomes complex. At worst, it tears the family apart.

While there are a few great successes of family controlled businesses, in general, families find it more desirable to sell the controlling interest and avoid any unpleasant conflicts. Public traded firms are great vehicles for insuring a peaceful transfer of power and wealth between generations.

DIVERSIFICATION

One of the primary reasons for families to sell their controlling interest in a family business is to achieve an adequate amount of investment diversification. Having all of one's eggs in a single basket is normally not a desirable investment strategy. In a dynamic competitive economy it is desirable for investors to be diversified.

While it is reasonable for a manager who is also an investor in a private equity firm to have excessive concentration of investments in the one stock, later when there is an opportunity to go public, this alternative has to receive serious consideration. The advantages of diversification for risk reduction are too large to ignore.

CAPITAL RAISING

A growing corporation will need to raise capital to take advantage of timely investment opportunities. A public traded firm has several distinct advantages when raising capital over the private equity firm. The most obvious advantage is the ability to issue common stock shares in the market. But even the issuance of debt is facilitated by the firm that has a market capitalization for its common stock.

A firm with publicly traded stock is required to file audited financial statements. These statements give potential lenders more confidence as to the reliability of the financial information.

MANAGEMENT AND OPTIONS

A publicly traded company has an advantage when trying to hire top management since it can offer stock options or the equivalent for a stock that has a readily determined market price. The private equity firm can contract with prospective managers, but the process is made more complex by the absence of a market price for the firm's stock.

MERGERS

A firm whose stock is widely held and publicly traded may become a merger target and the stockholders can envision a possible 30 percent to 40 percent takeover premium.

Now consider a minority shareholder in a private equity firm where the majority shareholders like to manage the firm. The likelihood of receiving a takeover premium from a merger is relatively low.

IRR OF THE LBO

Assume a firm is in the private equity business. To attract investors the firm must have a track record. The way a private equity firm establishes an enviable record is to take public firms private (private equity) and then after five to eight years take them public. After the firms go public the IRR of the equity investors is easily computed.

Assume a firm earns $100 after corporate tax at time 1 and is selling for $833 at time 0. The firm has a core value of $833 and this is the cost of the equity. A private equity fund acquires the firm and changes the $100 from a dividend to retained earnings. The capital gains tax rate is .20. The following facts apply to the firm's next four years of life if the firm will earn $100 of basic earnings each year, and earns .12 per year from any reinvestment of earnings. At the end of each year the basic core value is $833. Only the accumulated earnings are distributed (see Table 8.1).

The .12 corporate return is taxed at .2 so that for one year the private equity investor earns $.12(1 - .2) = .096$. For the four years, in each successive year the IRR increases. Since the firm's .12 return is larger than the after tax return the private equity investor earns, the tax deferral effect causes the IRR to increase.

If events happen as predicted the private equity firm at the end of four years will be able to report an internal rate of return (after investor tax) of .099. The before investor tax return is .12 if the firm value at time 4 is $1,309.93:

TABLE 8.1 IRR of the LBO

Horizon or Life	After Investor Tax Future Value of Retention If Firm Earns .12	Core (Basic) Value	Total Value	IRR
	$100(1 - .2)$	833	$ 913	.096
2	$(100 + 112).8 = 169.6$	833	1,002.6	.097
3	$(100 + 112 + 125.44).8 = 269.95$	833	1,102.95	.098
4	$(100 + 112 + 125.44 + 140.49).8 = 382.34$	833	1,215.34	.099

$$833(1 + IRR)^4 = 1,309.93$$
$$IRR = .12$$

For purposes of impressing investors the .12 is a better indicator of performance than the .099 after tax return. By substituting debt for some of the equity, the IRR can be increased above .12 if the debt costs less than .12.

CONCLUSIONS

We know that the majority of corporate business activity is conducted by firms that have publicly traded stock. Thus, despite all the advantages for private equity stock described previously the publicly traded corporation tends to win the organizational war. Why is this?

The primary advantage of the firm with publicly traded stock is the liquidity that is offered by this stock compared to private equity. In recent years companies have been shifting to more sensible dividend payout policies thus wiping out an important advantage for private equity capital (public firms no longer have to pay a cash dividend to be a competitive investment). Public capital firms offer many advantages compared to private equity firms when it comes to liquidity and a market determined price.

QUESTIONS AND PROBLEMS

1. What are the advantages of a firm with publicly traded stock?

2a. A firm's equity has a value of $604.

$$P = \frac{(1-t)D}{k-g} = \frac{(1-.396)100}{.12-.02} = \$604$$

Investors are taxed on ordinary income at .396 and on capital gains at .20. Assume that the firm's equity is purchased for $604. Instead of a $100 dividend the corporation will retain $125 per year and will earn .15 on reinvested funds. The reinvested earnings will add value (after 10 years) of $2,538.

Future value = $125B(10, .15)(1.15)^{10} = \$2,538$

Assuming the firm will have a value of $604 after the $2,538 is distributed, what is the present value of the firm (comparable to the $604 computed above)?

2b. What IRR is earned on the $604 investment?

CHAPTER 9

A Partial LBO: Almost Private Equity

A partial LBO is a financial strategy that avoids the pitfalls of an LBO, but at the same time achieves many of the objectives of an LBO. The strategy to follow is feasible and attractive.

An LBO led by management (the process can be called an MBO) may lead to a situation where competitive bidders are awakened (with management losing out) or where the bid moves up to a high level where it is difficult to make profits, let alone high profits. Also, the transaction costs of achieving the LBO may be high especially in terms of the time of the firm's top management and it can require that management make a larger personal financial commitment than management is comfortable making. Also management may end up with a small percentage of ownership.

Let us consider an alternative strategy, which is less disruptive and more effective (from management's perspective) and fairer (from the stockholders' perspective).

SHARE REPURCHASE

Let us assume a situation where a corporation is selling at five times cash flow and has a market capitalization for its stock of $500,000,000. The annual cash flow is $100,000,000. There are 10,000,000 shares outstanding.

The firm's strategy will be to spend the amount of capital needed to maintain the cash flow stream and use the remainder to repurchase shares of its common stock. Assume maintenance Cap-Ex is $20,000,000.

Of the 10,000,000 shares outstanding management owns 20 percent or 2,000,000. The stock is selling at $50 per share.

There is $80,000,000 of cash flow devoted to share repurchase and in the first year the firm will buy 1,600,000 shares at a price of $50 per share leaving 8,400,000 shares outstanding of which management (which did not sell) now owns 23.8 percent. Table 9.1 shows the management's ownership progression through six years. The firm's value at the end of each year is $500,000,000 (thanks to the maintenance Cap-Ex).

After only six years management will own $\dfrac{2,000,000}{3,513,000}$ or 56.9 percent assuming they do not sell any of their shares.

With a conventional LBO conducted with management as a participant, management will tend not to end up with a majority of the shares of stock. In the preceding example management owns 56.9 percent of the stock after only six years of the strategy.

If management increased its common stock investment by additional explicit investments, their percentage of ownership would increase even faster. The existence of stock options, restricted stock 401(k) plans, as well as explicit stock purchases by management would all result in a larger percentage of ownership.

A System of Equations

Instead of using a table to solve for management's percentage of ownership, we could use a system of equations or combine the

TABLE 9.1 Management's Ownership Progression

Year	Shares Outstanding	Price per Share	Shares Purchased with $80,000,000	New Number of Shares
1	10,000,000	$ 50.00	1,600,000	8,400,000
2	8,400,000	$ 59.52	1,344,000	7,056,000
3	7,056,000	$ 70.86	1,129,000	5,927,000
4	5,927,000	$ 84.36	948,000	4,979,000
5	4,979,000	$110.42	797,000	4,182,000
6	4,182,000	$119.56	669,000	3,513,000

equations into one equation. The advantage of the equations is that the assumptions can be readily changed and a new solution obtained.

Let p = the percentage of shares repurchased annually
g = the stock price growth rate and

$$g = \frac{p}{1-p} \tag{9.1}$$

P_i = the stock price at time i (the end of the year) and

$$P_i = (1 + g)^{i-1} P_1 \tag{9.2}$$

V = the value of the firm (the same at the end of each year)
N_i = the number of shares outstanding at the end of year i

$$N_i = \frac{V}{P_{i+1}} \tag{9.3}$$

M = the number of shares owned by management
Q_i = the percentage of the firm's shares owned by management at the end of year i

$$Q_i = \frac{M}{N_i} \tag{9.4}$$

For the example of the previous section assume we want to determine the percentage of shares owned by management at the end of year 6 (beginning of year 7).

The percentage of shares repurchased is

$$p = \frac{1,600,000}{10,000,000} = .16$$

and the stock price growth rate is

$$g = \frac{p}{1-p} = \frac{.16}{1-.16} = .1904761 \tag{9.1}$$

The price per share at the end of year 6 is ($P_1 = \$50$):

$$P_6 = (1 + g)^5 50 = \$119.56$$

The value of P_7 is

$$P_7 = (1 + g)^6 50 = \$142.33 \tag{9.2}$$

or equivalently

$$P_7 = (1 + g)P_6 = \$142.33$$

The number of shares outstanding at the end of year 6 is

$$N_6 = \frac{V}{P_7} = \frac{500,000,000}{142.33} = 3,513,000 \tag{9.3}$$

The percentage of shares owned by management at the end of year 6 is

$$Q_6 = \frac{M}{N_i} = \frac{2,000,000}{3,513,000} = 56.9\% \tag{9.4}$$

One Equation

The preceding system of equations can be replaced by one equation. Start with

$$Q_i = \frac{M}{N_i} \tag{9.4}$$

and substitute $\dfrac{V}{P_{i+1}}$ for N_i

$$Q_i = \frac{MP_{i+1}}{V}$$

Now substitute for P_{i+1}

$$Q_i = \frac{M(1+g)^i P_1}{V} \tag{9.5}$$

We could substitute for g

$$Q_i = \frac{M\left(1 + \dfrac{p}{1-p}\right)^i P_1}{V} \tag{9.6}$$

For the example

M = 2,000,000 shares
p = .16 or g = .1904761
i = 6
P_1 = $50
V = $500,000,000

and

$$Q_6 = \frac{2(1.1904761)^6\, 50}{500} = .569 \text{ or } 56.9\% \tag{9.6}$$

Now change the shares repurchased to p = .20 and g = .25

$$Q_6 = \frac{2(1.25)^6\, 50}{500} = .763 \text{ or } 76.3\%$$

Using equation (9.6) we can determine the sensitivity of the percentage of ownership to a change in any of the variables.

The Critical Assumptions

One critical assumption in arriving at the preceding results is the assumption that the stock was selling at five times the firm's cash flow. One can find publicly traded stocks selling at four times cash flow (the increase in percentage of ownership would be much larger). Five times cash flow is reasonable and leads to desirable results for management and investors following the partial LBO strategy.

The second critical assumption involved the amount of maintenance Cap-Ex. It was assumed that maintenance Cap-Ex equaled 20 percent of the cash flows. The magnitude was reasonable, but the logic of the model does not depend on this specific assumption.

The firm's market capitalization was kept constant at $500,000,000 at the end of each year. This is consistent with the fact that the firm's cash flow was kept constant at $100,000,000 ($80,000,000 after maintenance Cap-Ex). While the market capitalization can change even though the firm's cash flow stays constant, an assumption that the market capitalization is the same at the end of each year is reasonable.

Note that the nonmanagement shareholders are also benefited by the strategy being described. The market value of their remaining stock holdings increases from $50 per share to $120 at the end of the sixth year.

Use of Debt

To increase the ownership percentage of management the firm can issue debt and use the debt proceeds to repurchase shares.

Continuing the initial example, assume that the firm issues at the end of year 6 $200,000,000 of debt paying .07 interest. The before tax interest cost is $14,000,000 and $9,100,000 after tax.

Assuming a simple valuation model we have for the new firm value (V_L):

$$V_L = V_U + tB$$
$$= 500,000,000 + .35(200,000,000) = \$570,000,000$$

The new value of the stock is

$$S = V_L - B = 570,000,000 - 200,000,000 = \$370,000,000$$

Assume that the stock price per share before the debt issue is

$$\frac{420,000,000}{3,513,000} = \$119.56$$

or equivalently before the share repurchase at time 6:

$$\frac{500,000,000}{4,182,000} = \$119.56$$

With the \$200,000,000 of debt proceeds and a stock price of \$119.56 the firm can purchase 1,673,000 shares:

$$\frac{200,000,000}{119.56} = 1,673,000$$

leaving outstanding 3,513,000 − 1,673,000 = 1,840,000 shares. Management would own 100 percent of the outstanding shares and still be able to sell to the firm 160,000 of their holdings of 2,000,000 shares.

Instead of issuing the debt at the end of year 6, the debt could have been issued at time 0. This would affect all the subsequent calculations.

TWO OTHER FACTORS

There are two other factors that have the potential of enhancing management's percentage of ownership.

One is the firm awarding to management common stock shares or stock options. These awards will further increase the management's percentage of ownership.

Secondly, management can use their own resources to buy additional shares and accelerate the buyout process.

The Stock Price

The preceding example started with a value of the common stock of \$500,000,000 and this value was maintained with zero growth with the firm's having an annual \$20,000,000 capital expenditure. The stock prices for all time periods were obtained by dividing the \$500,000,000 end of year value by the outstanding shares. The stock price increased through time because of the decrease in outstanding shares.

Now assume that despite the absence of real growth the market decides the stock is more valuable because the market likes the financial strategy. In each year fewer shares will be purchased by the firm; thus the management's percentage of ownership will be less for each year than is illustrated.

While management is sad that it is making slower progress toward owning all the firm's stock, it might be happy that the stock it owns is now worth more.

One of the obvious objectives of management is to increase its wealth. If the stock price goes up a larger amount than is justified by the firm's basic operations, the wealth enhancement is partially achieved.

Stock Awards

Now assume 10 percent of the repurchased shares are awarded to management (1.6 percent of outstanding shares). All the numbers after year 1 change (see Table 9.2).

After six years management owns 65.4 percent (up from 56.9 percent).

TABLE 9.2 Ten Percent of Repurchased Shares Awarded to Management

End of Year	Shares Outstanding	Price per Share	Shares Repurchased	New Number of Shares	Owned by Management
1	10,000,000	$50.00	1,600,000	8,400,000 + 1,600,000 = 8,560,000	2,160,000
2	8,560,000	58.41	1,370,000	8,560,000 − 1,370,000 + 137,000 = 7,327,000	2,297,000
3	7,327,000	68.24	1,172,000	7,327,000 − 1,172,000 + 117,000 = 6,272,000	2,314,000
4	6,272,000	79.72	1,004,000	6,272,000 − 1,004,000 + 100,000 = 5,368,000	2,414,000
5	5,368,000	93.14	859,000	5,368,000 − 859,000 + 86,000 = 4,595,000	2,500,000
6	4,595,000	108.81	735,000	4,595,000 − 735,000 + 74,000 = 3,935,000	2,574,000

$$\frac{2,575,000}{3,935,000} = .654 \text{ or } 65.4\%$$

Issue Debt

Continuing the example with stock awards, now assume $200,000,000 of debt is issued at the end of year 6 and the proceeds are used to buy 1,838,000 shares at a price of $108.81.

$$\frac{200,000,000}{108.81} = 1,838,000 \text{ shares}$$

There are now 3,935,000 − 1,838,000 = 2,097,000 shares outstanding. Management owns 100 percent of the outstanding shares and can sell 2,574,000 − 2,097,000 = 477,000 shares back to the firm.

Is It Bad?

Suppose the stock market anticipates the partial LBO strategy and drives up the stock price. One possibility is that the larger stock price slows the LBO process. A second possibility is that management exploits the higher stock price by selling some of their shares.

So the larger stock price is not all bad though it does slow or alter the initial objective.

CONCLUSIONS

LBOs involving management have not always been successful. Where they are successful there is frequently resentment felt by the selling shareholders that they are being exploited by the insiders. Also, management ends up with a smaller percentage of ownership than it thinks it deserves.

The strategy recommended in this chapter bypasses these and other difficulties. The company repurchases shares and if management wants to gain control, they do not sell or they even can buy additional shares.

One of the primary advantages of the strategy of almost private equity is that the firm is always a public corporation. All investors (including management) have investment liquidity supplied by the capital markets.

The strategy offers some of the advantages of private equity without the disadvantages.

If desired, the proposed strategy can be enhanced by the firm issuing debt and using the debt proceeds for additional share repurchase, thus further increasing the percentage of outstanding shares owned by management.

QUESTIONS AND PROBLEMS

1. A corporation has a market capitalization of $400,000,000 and annual cash flow of $100,000,000. There are 20,000,000 shares outstanding. Maintenance Cap-Ex is $10,000,000. The stock price is $20.

   If cash flow in excess of maintenance Cap-Ex is used to repurchase shares, how many shares can be purchased?

   Prepare a table that shows management's progression of ownership for the next four years. Assume the firm's value remains at $400,000,000.

CHAPTER 10

Metromedia (1984)

In 1984 Metromedia was a diversified communications company with operations in the largest cities of the United States. The company had four different business segments.

Broadcasting Stations

Metromedia Television operated one network-affiliated and six independent affiliated television stations in seven major U.S. metropolitan areas. Metromedia Radio operated 7 AM and 6 FM radio stations in 10 major U.S. metropolitan areas and the Texas State Networks.

Telecommunications

Metromedia Telecommunications operated radio paging companies in nine major U.S. metropolitan areas.

Outdoor Advertising Management

Foster & Kleiser managed an outdoor advertising business in 21 major U.S. metropolitan areas.

Entertainment

Metromedia Producers Corporation produced and distributed television programs.
MetroTape supplied videotape production facilities and services.

Harlem Globetrotters, Inc. was a touring basketball entertainment team.

Ice Capades Inc. presented three touring shows and, under the names Ice Capades Chalets and Ice Capades Inc., operated 16 indoor ice skating rinks.

Over the 10 year period 1973 to 1983 net revenues grew at 15.7 percent per year and earnings by 26.3 percent. During 1983 the stock price hit a high of $56 and a low of $20.375. During the years 1982 and 1983 the number of shares of common stock were reduced from 37,200,000 to 29,600,000. At the end of 1983 long-term debt was $572.7 million and the book value of stockholders' equity was $198.5 million. A $.745 per share dividend was declared in 1983, up from $.550 in 1982 ($21.4 million in total, up from $18.3 million in 1982). During this time period the corporate tax rate was .46.

Net income in 1983 was $102,000,000, down from $309,000,000 in 1982 despite a 31 percent increase in net revenue. Operating income actually increased in 1983. There were $202,000,000 of gains on dispositions in 1982.

Despite its great 10 year record (the 5 year record was even better) the stock was not performing well. The firm's top management was very disappointed.

On November 23, 1983 the stock reached a 15-month low of $20.375. The company's 1983 annual report contained the following statement from John W. Kluge, Chairman of the Board, President, and Chief Executive Officer:

On December 6, Metromedia's Board of Directors received an offer from the office of the President and Boston Ventures Limited Partnership to take Metromedia private in a leveraged buyout transaction. Under the proposal, each share of Metromedia common stock would be converted into $30 cash and $22.50 principal amount of a new issue of subordinated discount debentures. The debentures would mature 14 years from issuance, would bear interest beginning in the sixth year at a rate of 16% per annum and would have the benefit of a sinking fund beginning in the tenth year. Because the debentures will not pay *interest for five years, it is expected that their market price will be substantially less than their principal amount. The proposal was approved by Metromedia's Board of Directors on January 31, 1984 but is subject to several conditions, including approval by Metromedia's stockholders, receipt of necessary regulatory approvals and obtaining cash financing of $1.4 billion for the purposes of making payments to stockholders, refinancing post merger operations.*

We are convinced that a business must be managed to maximize its value over the longer term, but we recognize that stock price considerations often prevent public companies from pursuing this course. Over the next several years, Metromedia expects to launch several cellular telephone systems. Growing demand for telecommunications services suggests that important long term opportunities exist in this exciting field. Longer term rewards likely will have near term costs, however, in the form of earnings penalties. Television programming offers additional opportunities, but these too may entail near term costs. While investment today doesn't guarantee long term rewards, its absences will surely preclude them.

As a private company, Metromedia will be better situated to take advantage of these opportunities. By focusing on long term rewards rather than near term expectations, we believe we can more effectively manage our growth.

Kluge's explanation is a classic description of the problem of a publicly traded company incurring short-term earnings disruptions in order to achieve long-term growth. In turn, the stock price went down. The solution chosen by management was to turn to private equity.

In June 1984, Metromedia executed the LBO (or more exactly, an MBO). The firm went private and the shareholders received $1.2 billion. To finance the LBO Metromedia borrowed $1.2 billion from banks and $125 million of preferred stock was sold to Prudential. The bank loans imposed a large number of restrictions and carried interest rates in excess of .14. The LBO group offered the shareholders $30 cash and a debenture with a present value of approximately $10. The stock in 1983, before the offer, sold at prices ranging from

$20 to $56 but during the fourth quarter of 1983 it only reached a high of $35.75 (see Table 10.1).

Some of the outstanding shares were held by the management participating in the LBO and would not be sold (Kluge owned 26 percent of the firm's common stock).

Some of the presently outstanding debt would also have to be paid.

The $22.50 face value debt maturing in 14 years given to the shareholders paid .16 or $3.60 per year starting in year 7. Assuming a .15 discount rate we have:

$$22.50(1.15)^{-14} = 22.50(.1413) \qquad \$\ 3.18$$
$$3.60B(8, .15)(1.15)^{-6} \qquad\qquad \underline{6.98}$$
$$\underline{\underline{\$10.16}}$$

Boston Ventures contributed $10 million of capital in return for nonvoting common stock.

Metromedia's 1983 annual report shows total assets of $1.3 billion and stock equity of $198,470,000 for the end of 1983.

The LBO increased Kluge's ownership of equity from 26 percent before the LBO to 75.5 percent. The amount of equity also changed. For Kluge to achieve a 75.5 percent ownership of the equity highlighted the brilliance of the man.

The *Wall Street Journal* headline (November 30, 1984) was "Metromedia Unit Issues $1.9 billion of 'Junk Bonds'; Offering Called Largest." The bonds were sold to institutional investors by Drexel Burnham Lambert. The offering sold out in two hours.

The debt offering is as shown in Table 10.2.

After the LBO was completed, pieces of the firm were sold in 1985 and 1986 (see Table 10.3).

TABLE 10.1   Total Value to Shareholders

Shares outstanding	29,584,000
Cash	× $30
Total cash needed	$ 887,520,000
$22.50 Debt ($10 value)	$ 295,840,000
Total value to shareholders	$1,183,360,000

TABLE 10.2 The Debt Offering

$ 960	million of serial zero-coupon notes (interest rates of 13.75% to 15.25%) Issued at $397.5 million. Maturing from 1988 to 1993
$ 225	million of 15-year debentures yielding 15.756%
$ 335	million of 12-year exchangeable (at company's option into fixed rate notes during 1996) variable rate debentures
$ 400	million of 18-year floating rate participating debentures (tied to cash flow growth)
$1,920	million

TABLE 10.3 Pieces Sold in 1985 and 1986

7 TV stations	$ 2.00 billion
Outdoor advertising	.71
Entertainment	.03
Radio (9 stations)	.29
Cellular and paging	1.65
	$ 4.68 billion

In execution, the sum of the parts exceeded the value established by the market on the whole firm.

QUESTIONS AND PROBLEMS

1. How much debt did Metromedia issue on November 30, 1984?

2. Was the total outlay of $1,183,000,000 to the shareholders too high? Assume the stock was selling no higher than $35.75 before the offer. What value do you place on Metromedia's equity?

3. As a stockbroker would you tender your stock for an offer price of $40?

4. How was value added?

5. If you were structuring the bank debt or the replacement debt, what would you (the lender) change?

6. What was the value of Kluge's equity immediately before the LBO? Assume a stock value of $20.38 per share.

7. Assume a firm value of $1,228,000,000 after the LBO (before any sale of pieces). What was the value of Kluge's equity?

CHAPTER 11

LBO of RJR Nabisco (1988)*

R JR Nabisco was among the largest consumer product companies in the world in 1988. The company was a leader in each of its two lines of business, tobacco and food. In the United States its tobacco business was the second largest producer of cigarettes and its packaged food business was the largest manufacturer of cookies and crackers. Both tobacco and food products were sold around the world under a variety of well-recognized brand names.

Activities of RJR Tobacco Company were confined to the tobacco industry until the 1960s, when diversification led to investments in transportation, energy, and food. With the acquisition of Del Monte in 1979, the Company began to concentrate its diversification efforts toward consumer products. The Company's strategy led to the acquisition of Heublein, Inc. in 1982 and culminated in the acquisition, at a total cost of $4.9 billion, of Nabisco in 1985. In 1984 the Company spun off to its stockholders its transportation business, conducted by Sea-Land Corporation, and sold its energy business. In 1986 the Company divested several operations not considered to be within its consumer products focus, including its quick service restaurant businesses, conducted principally by Kentucky Fried Chicken Corporation. During 1987 the Company sold its spirits and wines businesses, conducted principally by Heublein, Inc.

The RJR stock price was between $47 and $55 during the third quarter of 1988. For simplicity assume a $50 stock price

---

*For the classic and colorful story of the RJR Nabisco LBO see B. Burrough and J. Helyar, *Barbarians at the Gate*, Harper & Row, New York, 1990. Rich Owens helped prepare an earlier version of this case.

before the play begins and 224,000,000 shares outstanding. The market capitalization was $11.2 billion. The corporate tax rate was .34. A reasonable debt rate for a highly levered firm was .12. For 1988 RJR's cash flows from operations were $1,480 million. The income taxes paid were $682 million and interest paid was $486 million (long-term debt was $4,975 million). The net income applicable to common stock was $1.378 billion and income to its total equity was $1.393 billion. Cash dividends on common stock were $475 million.

BACKGROUND ON RJR NABISCO

On September 10, 1985 RJ Reynolds Tobacco Company had bought Nabisco Brands, Inc. for $4.9 billion, thereby forming RJR Nabisco, Inc. The corporation's two major subsidiaries included RJ Reynolds (Tobacco) and Nabisco Brands, Inc. During 1988, its food division accounted for approximately 58 percent ($9.9 billion) of total sales while the tobacco division accounted for the remainder ($7.1 billion).

BACKGROUND OF THE LEVERAGED BUYOUT

In September 1988, Henry R. Kravis of Kohlberg Kravis Roberts & Co. (KKR) discussed with F. Ross Johnson, CEO of RJR Nabisco, the possibilities of organizing, with Johnson's cooperation, a leveraged buyout (LBO) of RJR Nabisco. The next month during an RJR Nabisco board of directors meeting, Johnson announced that he and a group of senior managers together with Shearson Lehman Hutton Inc. (Shearson) intended to take the company private using a leveraged buyout. The tentative price was set at $75 per share. Based on a $50 stock price this was a .50 premium, a reasonable premium.

When RJR's board of directors announced the Management Group's offer, a Special Committee was formed to study the offer and alternatives. Financial advisors (Dillon, Read & Co. Inc. and Lazard Freres & Co.) and legal advisors (Skadden, Arps, Slate, Meagher & Flom) were retained by the Committee.

On October 24 KKR announced its leveraged buyout plan to acquire RJR shares at a price of $90. KKR expressed its desire to keep negotiations friendly and called for senior members of management, including Johnson, to join KKR's acquisition efforts. KKR began its tender offer for up to 87 percent of the outstanding shares at $90 per share. KKR also announced its intention to exchange untendered shares for new securities in a second step. Confidentiality agreements between KKR and the Special Committee were executed allowing KKR access to confidential information about the company. The Committee set the ground rules whereby interested parties were to submit the potential purchaser's highest offer by 5:00 P.M., November 18, 1988.

By the November 18 deadline, the management group offered to buy 175 million shares at $100 cash per share. Shares not tendered or accepted would be exchanged in a "cram down merger" for $56 cash, preferred stock, and convertible preferred stock. There were an average of 233 million shares outstanding during 1988. The Management Group hired Salomon Brothers Inc. as an advisor.

KKR offered $94 cash for 177,565,220 shares. Any untendered shares would be exchanged for 2.1786 shares of preferred stock and senior convertible debentures. The total value of the package was estimated to be $94 per share.

The Committee granted the bidders additional time to work out the details of their proposals by extending the deadline from November 18 to November 29, 1988. On that date the Committee accepted revised bids from management and from KKR. Management offered $112 cash and a package of securities (PIK preferred, convertible preferred stock) with an estimated value of $112. PIKs are securities which give the issuer a choice.

KKR offered $109 cash for up to 165,509,015 shares of common stock (representing approximately 74 percent of the unrestricted shares of common stock prior to the tender offer). The security package (PIK preferred stock and convertible debentures) also had an estimated value of $109. Cash of $108 was offered for any and all shares of preferred stock.

On November 30 the Committee also considered the feasibility of a leveraged recapitalization or a possible breakup. Because such measures would not be expected to create more value to shareholders than $109, the ideas were abandoned. The Committee's advisors discounted the PIK preferred stock of the Management Group's offer by approximately $2 per share and the convertible preferred stock by $1.50, resulting in a valuation of $108.50 for the offer of the Management Group.

Likewise, KKR's PIK preferred was discounted resulting in a valuation of $108.50. The Committee's advisors concluded that both offers were "substantially equivalent." After considering all relevant factors, by unanimous vote of the Committee, KKR's final bid was accepted.

The Management Group notified the Committee that their efforts, in conjunction with Shearson and Salomon Brothers, to buy out the company were terminated.

In January 1989 the Federal Trade Commission found no antitrust violations and approved the acquisition of the company by KKR. The Delaware Chancery Court denied a motion by a shareholder group that the court enjoin the tender offer on grounds that the Committee and the board of directors had breached their fiduciary duty by accepting KKR's marginally lower bid (relative to the Management Group's bid).

KKR's tender offer expired in February after KKR acquired 165,509,015 shares of common stock (approximately 74 percent of those unrestricted and outstanding shares before the tender offer) for $109 cash and 1,196,652 shares of preferred stock for $108 cash. The total amount paid in cash was $18,169,700,000.

Structure of the Deal

> Cash for 165,509,015 shares of common stock at $109 per share
>
> Cash for 1,196,652 shares of preferred stock at $108 per share

$109 × 165,509,015 shares $18,040,442,635
$108 × 1,196,652 shares   129,238,416
    Total $18,169,681,051

Each untendered share of common stock (shares in excess of 165,509,015 shares) received the following:

	Estimated Value
2.8030 shares of PIK preferred stock ($25 per share)	$ 70.08
Amount of senior convertible debentures	$ 38.92
	$109.00

The PIK preferred stock:

- Dividends paid "in kind" for first six years
- Initial floating dividend rate 14.7%
- Dividend rate to float 550 basis points over highest of:
   1. 3-month Treasury bill rate
   2. 10-year Treasury bond rate
   3. 30-year Treasury bond rate
- Dividend rate floor 12.625%; ceiling 16.625%
- Dividend rate reset to a fixed rate to trade at par at earlier of:
   1. One year following refinancing of bridge loans or
   2. Two years after tender offer closed
- Stock redeemable at any time after merger

The senior convertible debentures

- May be converted to common stock at the end of four years
- Payment "in kind" or cash for 10 years, then cash distributions thereafter
- Interest rate reset to trade at par at earlier of:
   1. One year following refinancing of bridge loans
   2. Two years after tender offer closed

■ Initial interest rate set at approximately 14.7%
■ Maturity in 20 years
■ Optional redemption by RJR at any time after fourth year

The total capital needed to accomplish the cash component of the LBO is $18.925 billion.

Purchase of common stock	$18.040 billion
Purchase of preferred stock	.129
Fees and expense	.756
	$18.925 billion

The cash tender offer was financed by those shown in Table 11.1.

The cash tender offer part of the acquisition was financed with .92 debt and .08 equity. Of course, some of the equity may have been financed with debt.

In addition, there were the PIK preferred and the senior convertible debentures issued in exchange for the common stock not exchanged for cash.

The bank debt was refinanced shortly after the LBO with a bank bridge facility ($7.5 billion), senior convertible debentures ($2.3 billion), and preferred stock ($4.1 billion).

TABLE 11.1   The Cash Tender Offer

Bank	$11.925 billion	.63
Increasing rate notes (IRN)	1.250	.07
Subordinated IRN	3.750	.20
Partnership debt	.500	.02
Equity	1.500	.08
	$18.925 billion	1.00

QUESTIONS AND PROBLEMS

For the following questions assume that KKR does not bring any significant synergies or efficiencies. The only gains are from financial strategies.

1. What is the maximum value KKR should bid assuming the $50 stock price accurately reflects the firm's value before the LBO competition starts?

2. What is the maximum amount of .12 debt (incremental) that RJR can support? What would be the effect of a higher interest rate?

3. How much did KKR pay for the common stock of RJR?

4. Did KKR overpay for RJR? Did KKR win or lose?

CHAPTER 12

Marietta Corporation (1994–1996)

Marietta is primarily engaged in the design, manufacture, packaging, marketing, and distribution of guest amenity products to the travel and lodging industry in the United States and abroad, and provides customized "sample-size" and "unit-of-use" packaging products and services to companies in the toiletries, cosmetics, pharmaceutical, and household products industries.

Parent, a corporation controlled by Barry W. Florescue, was organized under the laws of the State of Delaware for the purpose of merging with Marietta (essentially acquiring Marietta). Newco, a wholly-owned subsidiary of Parent, was organized under the laws of the State of New York for the purpose of the merger. Newco would be the vehicle for the acquisition.

Mr. Florescue commenced acquiring shares in February 1994. On October 3, 1994, Mr. Florescue filed a schedule with the SEC indicating that as of such date he beneficially owned an aggregate of 186,165 shares, representing approximately 5.2 percent of the then issued and outstanding shares. The report stated that Mr. Florescue had purchased such shares for investment purposes.

On January 17, 1995, Dickstein Partners, Inc. (Dickstein) made an unsolicited conditional proposal to acquire by means of a cash merger all outstanding shares at a price of $11 per share (the Dickstein Proposal). Dickstein's Schedule 13D stated that Dickstein beneficially owned an aggregate of 526,000 shares, representing approximately 14.6 percent of the then outstanding shares and that on January 19, 1995, Dickstein had filed preliminary proxy materials with the SEC indicating Dickstein's intention, at the company's 1995 annual meeting of shareholders, to propose a slate of its own directors.

The Schedule 13D also stated that the nominees of Dickstein "would be committed to a program of offering the company for sale, and selling the Company, to the buyer who is willing to pay the highest price, so long as the price is at least $11 per share."

Following the announcement of the Dickstein Proposal, the board retained the services of a financial advisor. After interviewing four nationally regarded investment advisors, on January 25, 1995 the board authorized the exclusive engagement of Goldman Sachs.

On March 13, 1995, the company, after consultation with its legal and financial advisors, announced that the board had unanimously rejected the Dickstein Proposal as inadequate and not in the best interests of the company and its shareholders. In light of the fact that such unsolicited proposal was subject to financing and due diligence conditions, as well as the negotiation of definitive agreements, the board could not conclude that the Dickstein Proposal was a bona fide offer. In addition, the board was not prepared to accept any offers for the purchase of the company without exploring a sales process that it believed would result in the shareholders' receiving the highest price for their shares.

As part of the process to maximize shareholder value, the company received an indication from a banking institution of preliminary interest in, for a due diligence fee, exploring a debt financing with the company in an amount to be agreed upon. Such financing would be used to enable the company to declare a special dividend to all shareholders or finance a self-tender by the company of some of its outstanding shares. The board did not pursue these alternatives because it believed that it would not be in the best interest of shareholders to declare a special dividend or conduct a self-tender for its shares. The board believed that the financing of such alternatives would require the company to incur significant indebtedness at a time when it was experiencing financial and operating uncertainty. Further, the board was concerned that a special dividend or self-tender would adversely affect the market liquidity of shares and could limit institutional research coverage of the company. In addition, the board believed that it would be difficult to secure financing for such alternatives upon acceptable terms. The board believed that a sale of the company was the alternative that would maximize shareholder value and determined to pursue the sales process to its conclusion before considering a special dividend, self-tender, or any other financial alternative.

On June 22, 1995, the board met to discuss a Second Dickstein Proposal. At the meeting the board determined that based upon the various conditions contained in each proposal, accepting either proposal would create an obligation of the company to sell itself to a purchaser without concurrently obligating the purchaser to consummate such purchase.

With respect to the Second Dickstein Proposal, the board was particularly concerned that Dickstein had not provided adequate assurance of its ability to finance the acquisition. Moreover, the board believed that if the company accepted the Second Dickstein Proposal, the failure by the company to achieve the specified levels of operating income during the company's third and fourth 1995 fiscal quarters would have resulted in an obligation by the company to pay a substantial breakup fee to Dickstein and, if the agreement were so terminated for this reason, it would have an adverse impact on the value of the shares and on the process of maximizing shareholder value. Based upon the company's then most recent projections for the remainder of the 1995 fiscal year, the board was concerned about the company's ability to achieve the required levels of operating income. In fact, the company did not achieve such levels of operating income.

With respect to the Florescue Proposal, the board believed that Mr. Florescue had also not provided adequate assurance of his ability to finance the acquisition of the company and that the due diligence condition in such proposal was not appropriate.

Despite these reservations the company authorized its representatives to continue discussions with Dickstein and Mr. Florescue to determine if more reasonable terms could be agreed to which in the board's opinion would be in the best interest of all shareholders. The board further determined that it would recommend to shareholders that the highest offer containing reasonable conditions be accepted, provided that such offer was at least $11 per share in cash for all shares and that the bidder demonstrate to the board that it had the financial ability to complete the transaction.

On August 3, 1995, the company announced its financial results for the third fiscal quarter. Net sales for the third quarter, as compared to the third quarter of the company's prior fiscal year, had declined 1.2 percent, and the company's net loss for the third quarter was $457,124 ($0.13 per share) as compared to net income of $785,574 ($.22 per share) in the third quarter of fiscal 1994. The company indicated that the third quarter of fiscal 1995 was negatively affected by approximately $652,000 in legal and professional fees incurred primarily in connection with the matters relating to the Dickstein Proposal. Other significant factors contributing to the results for the third quarter were higher than anticipated materials costs. The company also announced increased prices effective August 15, 1995, to offset the highest material costs and stated that it expected that capital expenditures made by the company during fiscal year 1995 would result in improved productivity and efficiency at its soap manufacturing facility.

On August 14, 1995, the company distributed its proxy statement to the company's shareholders. On August 15, 1995, Dickstein distributed a proxy statement to the company's shareholders, setting forth a slate of nominees for election as directors of the company, who, if elected, indicated that they were committed to seeking to implement the Self-Tender Proposal.

On August 21, 1995, Mr. Florescue offered $10 per share in cash. Mr. Florescue stated that in light of the company's financial results for the third fiscal quarter he was unwilling to resubmit an offer of $12.30 per share. On August 23, 1995, the board was advised on the status of negotiations and the material issues on which the company should continue discussions with Mr. Florescue with a view toward entering into the Merger Agreement. On August 24, 1995 and August 25, 1995, representatives of the company and Mr. Florescue negotiated a resolution of all issues on which the parties were not in agreement. During such negotiations, Mr. Florescue increased his offer to $10.25 per share in cash.

On August 27, 1995, the company announced that it had signed the Merger Agreement.

On August 30, 1995, Dickstein announced that, in light of the

Merger Agreement, it was withdrawing its slate of nominees for consideration by the company's shareholders.

The decision by the board to enter into the Merger Agreement reflected, in part, an assessment of the risks and potential benefits of other strategic and financial alternatives available to the company as compared with the risks and benefits of a transaction that would offer all shareholders of the company (other than Parent and its affiliates) the opportunity to receive a premium over the market price for their shares. In its deliberations, the board considered a number of factors, including (1) the board's knowledge of the business, operations, properties, assets, financial condition, operating results, and prospects of the company; (2) the fact that the offer made by Parent resulted from an extensive, publicly announced sales process for the company; and (3) the terms of the Merger Agreement. The board also believed that the sale process it conducted had allowed for the broadest possible exposure of the company to potential buyers. As previously disclosed, contact was made with more than 100 parties, and the company's management along with Goldman Sachs actively participated in facilitating the sale process. Strategic as well as financial buyers were contacted by Goldman Sachs. The board believed that the most accurate indication of the company's value was its value as a going concern and that the sales process yielded the best indication of the company's value as a going concern.

The board also considered (1) the fact that the price of $10.25 per share will be paid in cash; (2) the fact that it is a condition to the obligation of the company to consummate the merger that it receive an opinion from Goldman Sachs as to the fairness of $10.25 per share in cash; and (3) possible alternatives to the merger, including continuing to operate the company as an independent public company, initiating a self-tender, as well as the impact, short-term and long-term, of such alternatives on shareholder value. With regard to the possible alternatives considered, the board believed that it would not be in the best interest of the company's shareholders to declare a special dividend or conduct a self-tender for its shares since such alternatives would require the company to incur significant indebtedness that might weaken the company's financial position. In addition, in light of the company's uncertain operating and financial prospects, the board did not deem it advisable to cause the company to incur significant debt. Further, the board was concerned that a special dividend or self-tender would adversely affect the market liquidity of the shares and could limit institutional research coverage of the company. Accordingly, in view of the factors the board concluded that there could be no assurance that the company's shareholders would be able to realize any greater value for their shares in any of the other transactions considered by the board.

Goldman Sachs delivered to the board its written opinion to the effect that, based on various considerations and assumptions, $10.25 per share in cash is fair to the holders of shares (other than Parent and its affiliates). In its opinion, Goldman Sachs noted that consummation of the merger is subject to certain conditions, including the securing by Parent of financing necessary to consummate the merger.

The following is a summary of certain of the financial analyses reviewed by Goldman Sachs with the board on November 27, 1995.

(I) Analysis of the Per Share Price. Goldman Sachs prepared a financial analysis of the merger and calculated the aggregate consideration and various financial multiples based upon the cash consideration of $10.25 per share, using historical results for the company's fiscal year 1995 and management projections for the company's fiscal years 1996 and 1997.

(II) Selected Companies Analysis. Goldman Sachs reviewed and compared certain financial information relating to the company to corresponding financial information, ratios, and public market multiples for the sole publicly traded guest amenity firm identified (Guest Supply, Inc.) and other selected publicly traded custom packaging companies. The selected companies were chosen because they are publicly traded companies with operations that, for purposes of analysis, may be considered similar to the company; however, given the company's specialized operations, no company used in the analysis as a comparison is identical to the company. Goldman Sachs calculated and compared various financial multiples and ratios. The multiples of each of the selected companies were based on the most recent publicly available information. With respect to the selected companies, Goldman Sachs considered leveraged market

capitalization (market value of common equity plus debt less cash) as a multiple of the last 12 months (LTM) sales, as a multiple of LTM EBITDA and as a multiple of LTM EBIT. Many of the companies analyzed have higher IBES long-term growth rates than the growth projected for the company by its management. IBES is a data service that monitors and publishes a compilation of earnings estimates produced by selected research analysts on companies of interest to investors.

(III) Selected Transaction Analysis. Goldman Sachs analyzed certain information relating to selected transactions in the specialty packaging industry since 1986 (the Selected Transactions). Given the company's specialized operations, no transaction used in the analysis as a comparison is identical to the transaction considered. The analysis indicated that the price of $10.25 per share being paid in the merger was, as a multiple of LTM sales, at the low end of the range and, as a multiple of LTM EBIT and LTM EBITDA, at the high end of the range in comparison with the Selected Transactions.

(IV) Discounted Cash Flow Analysis. Goldman Sachs performed a discounted cash flow analysis using projections provided by the management of the company. Free cash flow represents the amount of cash generated and available for principal, interest, and dividend payments after providing for ongoing business operations and taxes. Goldman Sachs aggregated (x) the present value of the projected free cash flows over the five year period from 4x to 5x projected 2000 EBITDA. These terminal values as well as the projected cash flows for the years 1996 through 2000 were then discounted to the present value using discount rates from 11 percent to 15 percent. Based upon the foregoing discounted cash flow analysis, the net present value per share ranged from $9.17 to $14.57.

Goldman Sachs also performed a sensitivity analysis on the discounted cash flow analysis. Assuming a fixed terminal value multiple of 5x projected 2000 EBITDA and a 14 percent discount rate, projected sales growth was varied by a range of (2.0) percent to 2.0 percent and EBIT margins were varied by a range of (3.0) percent to 2.0 percent. Based upon the sensitivity analysis, the net present value per share of common stock ranged from $7.43 to $14.26, which compare to the $11.22 value at the illustrative terminal value and discount rate of 5x and 15 percent, respectively.

The discounted cash flow analysis is an analysis that should be considered with the recognition that this analysis is most applicable to a strategic/corporate potential acquirer and with the recognition that an acquirer typically would not look to pay the full discounted cash flow valuation of a company. Paying the full valuation would equate to an acquirer's transferring full value to selling stockholders while retaining no projected value and full risk for the acquirer's stockholders.

(V) Leveraged Buyout Analysis. Goldman Sachs performed a leveraged buyout analysis using projections provided by the management of the company and based upon the cash consideration of $10.25 per share. Coverage ratios, cash available to service principal repayment and equity returns were calculated using a capital structure consisting of $25 million in senior debt, $3.2 million in revolving debt, and $8 million in debt. The coverage ratios, defined as EBITDA less capital expenditures divided by interest expense, were 1.7x, 2.3x, and 3.1x for estimated 1996, 1998, and 2000. Cash available to service principal repayment was $0.0, $0.0, $1.0, and $7.1 for estimated 1996, 1998, 2000, and 2002. Equity returns in estimated 2000 were 34.6 percent and 42.5 percent given a 5x EBITDA exit value and a 6x EBITDA exit value, respectively.

Prior to the foregoing presentation, in the late summer of 1995, Goldman Sachs updated a share repurchase analysis it had earlier prepared (updated for the most recent management projections). The analysis indicated that a repurchase of shares at a price of $10.25 per share in varying aggregate amounts of $5.8, $10, $16, and $25 million would result in pro forma projected fiscal 1996 EBIT-Cap Ex ratios (earnings before interest and taxes, less expenditures divided by net interest and other expense) of 2.4, 1.2, 0.7, and 0.4, respectively. In all scenarios based on 1995 projected earnings, the repurchases would have been dilutive and in all scenarios, based on 1996 projected earnings, the repurchases would have been dilutive and coverage ratios associated with a major share repurchase program (or, alternatively, payment of a significant special dividend), particularly those ratios associated with the larger transactions, suggest that such transactions would be difficult to finance. Prior to entering into the Merger Agreement, the board of Marietta concluded that it would be unwise to incur significant amounts of indebtedness to finance a significant share repurchase or special dividend in light of recent operating results.

SOURCES AND USES OF FUNDS

The sources and uses of the funds constituting the financing and the estimated fees and expenses incurred or to be incurred by the company, Newco, and Parent in connection with the merger are approximately as shown in Table 12.1.

TABLE 12.1 Sources and Uses of Funds

Sources of Funds	
Issuance of subordinated debt	$15,000,000
Amount available under revolving credit facility	14,000,000
Issuance of term loan	6,000,000
Contribution of cash and common stock	7,500,000
Cash on hand	8,800,000
Total sources	$51,300,000

Uses of Funds	
Purchase of company capital stock (1)	$37,300,000
Refinance company debt	1,825,000
Post-merger working capital	7,355,000
Advisory fees (2)	3,000,000
Bank and subordinated debt financing fees and expenses	800,000
Legal fees and expenses	750,000
Accounting fees and expenses	125,000
Commission filing fees	6,800
Printing and mailing expenses	100,000
Exchange agent fees and expenses	3,200
Proxy solicitation fees and expenses	10,000
Miscellaneous expenses	25,000
Total uses	$51,300,000

(1) Includes payment for all outstanding shares other than those owned by the parent or its affiliates plus payments in settlement of outstanding employee stock options in accordance with the Merger Agreement.
(2) Includes the fees and estimated expenses of Goldman Sachs.

MARKET PRICES OF SHARES

Table 12.2 sets forth, for the periods indicated, the range of high and low closing prices per share.

On August 25, 1995, the last full trading day before the public announcement of the execution of the Merger Agreement, the last reported sale price per share as reported by the NASDAQ was $9.

During the company's last five fiscal years, no dividends have been declared by the company with respect to shares (see Tables 12.3 and 12.4).

TABLE 12.2   Range of High and Low Closing Prices
per Share

	High	Low
Year Ended October 1, 1994		
First Quarter	$8^{1}/_{2}$	$6^{1}/_{2}$
Second Quarter	9	6
Third Quarter	$9^{3}/_{8}$	$7^{1}/_{2}$
Fourth Quarter	$9^{1}/_{2}$	$7^{1}/_{2}$
Year Ended September 30, 1995		
First Quarter	$8^{3}/_{4}$	$6^{3}/_{4}$
Second Quarter	$11^{1}/_{2}$	$7^{1}/_{2}$
Third Quarter	$11^{1}/_{8}$	$9^{1}/_{2}$
Fourth Quarter	$10^{1}/_{2}$	7
Year Ended September 28, 1996		
First Quarter	$9^{1}/_{4}$	$7^{3}/_{4}$

TABLE 12.3   Marietta Corporation and Subsidiaries Consolidated Balance Sheets*

	Sept. 30, 1995
Total Current Assets	$32,265,010
Property, plant and equipment, net	23,162,584
Restricted cash	2,700,000
Marketable securities	2,432,050
Excess of cover over net assets acquired, net	3,202,052
Other assets	368,888
Total Assets	$64,130,584
Total Current Liabilities	$ 8,643,242
Long-term debt, less current maturities	6,514,335
Convertible subordinated note	278,040
Deferred tax liability	2,197,228
Total Liabilities	$17,632,845
Total Shareholders' Equity	46,497,739
Total Liabilities and Shareholders' Equity	$64,130,584

*Based on information from Marietta's Form 10-Q for the quarterly period ended December 30, 1995.

TABLE 12.4   Marietta Corporation Consolidated Statements of Operation (Unaudited)

	Three Months Ended December 30, 1995
Operating income	$ 608,908
Other income (expense), net	106,333
Income before income taxes	715,241
Income tax provision	307,399
Net income	$ 407,852
Earnings per share	$ 0.11
Weighted average shares and common share equivalents	$3,621,516

QUESTIONS AND PROBLEMS

1. Using just the balance sheet, determine the value of the Marietta Corporation as of September 30, 1995. Assume Marietta debt yields .10 contractually and the current rate for equivalent risk debt is .06.

2. As a stockholder, would you accept the $10.25 offer? Assume there are 3,621,000 shares outstanding and that the calculations are based on the information from the quarter ending December 30, 1995.

3. If you acquired Marietta, what would be your capital structure? What would be the value per share?

4. What should the management and Board of Directors have done, given the $11 offer?

CHAPTER 13

The Managerial Buyout of United States Can Company (2000)

U.S. Can is a manufacturer of steel containers for household products, automotive parts, paint, industrial products, and specialty products in the United States and Europe, as well as plastic containers in the United States and food cans in Europe. Its main competitors are Crown Cork and Seal and B Way Corporation.

During the year ending December 31, 1999 the U.S. Can Company earned $21,156,000 for common stock or $1.65 per share (full diluted).

On July 2, 2000 an LBO group headed by Berkshire Partners (a private equity firm) offered to buy U.S. Can's common stock for $276.9 million. The acquiring corporation (Pac Packaging Acquisition Corporation) was formed by Paul Jones, Chairman and CEO and John Workman, CFO of U.S. Can and Berkshire Partners.

The holders of shares of U.S. Can common stock will receive $20 per share in cash (except the rollover stockholders). For 1999 the stock's high price was $25.625 and the low was $13.750. For the first half of 2000 the low was $12.50 and the high was $21.25. On March 21, 2000 (the last trading day before U.S. Can announced to the public the initial recapitalization proposal) the low was $14.562 and the high was $15.000. The $20 offer price on March 21 was a .333 premium to that day's high.

U.S. Can had never paid a cash dividend and had no intention of paying one.

The rollover stockholders included certain members of U.S.

Can's senior management and other insider shareholders. Ordinary shareholders could not roll over.

The EBITDA for the year ending June 30, 2000 was $106.4 million. The ratio of common stock purchase price to EBITDA was 2.6.

$$\text{Multiplier} = \frac{276.9}{106.4} = 2.6$$

Adding $322.1 million of total debt to the numerator we have

$$\text{Multiplier} = \frac{276.9 + 322.1}{106.4} = 5.63$$

The above debt excludes the $44,500,000 of fees and expenses associated with the LBO.

Affiliates of Berkshire Partners will own approximately 73 percent of U.S. Can's common stock and 84.31 percent of the preferred stock after the recapitalization. Paul Jones (CEO) will own 3.5 percent of the outstanding shares and John Workman 1.75 percent. Management will own 9 percent of common stock equity and 3 percent of total equity. Before the LBO they owned .54 percent of the total equity.

U.S. Can will pay cash bonuses of $697,500 to Mr. Jones and $309,000 to Mr. Workman (and $676,200 to other members of management) to help them finance the purchases of common stock.

The merger agreement restricted U.S. Can's ability to initiate, solicit, or encourage any competing merger or acquisition inquiries. An investment bank did try to generate competitive offers (it was unsuccessful).

The investors receiving $20 cash per share have a taxable transaction if their tax basis is less than $20. Following the recapitalization there will be no trading market for U.S. Can's shares.

Mr. Jones' investment will increase from $646,000 to $1,866,667 after the recapitalization and Mr. Workman's from $190,000 to $933,333.

Jones and Workman first met with bankers to discuss an LBO, or equivalent transaction, on February 2, 2000. The recapitalization was announced to the public after trading on March 21, 2000.

Salomon Smith Barney (hired by U.S. Can) used a discounted cash flow analysis to obtain a value between $18 and $22 per share. They also obtained an EBITDA multiple ranging from 5.6 to 6.2 depending on the amount of debt assumption.

Rexam acquired American National Can in April 2000 at 5.68 times EBITDA and 8.72 times EBIT.

For a list of comparable firms Lazard (hired by U.S. Can's board of directors) found that the high multiples for the last 12 months were 6.6 times EBITDA, 11.3 times EBIT, and 9 times earnings. Using a discounted cash flow analysis Lazard found an equity value of $15.93 to $28.38 for U.S. Can stock. Lazard used a discount rate of 11 percent to 13 percent and terminal EBITDA multiples of 4.5 to 6.0. Lazard also computed the median premium paid for recent acquisitions of comparable firms to be .296 based on the price one day prior to announcement of the transaction.

Lazard also did an LBO analysis assuming IRRs of 20 percent to 30 percent and terminal EBITDA multiples of between 4.5 and 6.0. They found an LBO purchaser might be willing to pay between $18 and $22 per share and still earn acceptable returns.

U.S. Can's management made the projections shown in Table 13.1.

The reasons offered for the recapitalization in the proxy statement are:

Despite U.S. Can having shown strong earnings growth and substantially reducing debt in 1998 and 1999, by early 2000 U.S. Can's stock price had generally declined to below the levels at which it was trading at the beginning of 1998. Each of the affiliates of U.S. Can that is participating in the recapitalization believes that this trend has prevented stockholders

TABLE 13.1 U.S. Can's Management Projections

	Year Ended December 31 (in millions)				
	2000	2001	2002	2003	2004
Net Income	23.3	29.6	36.0	40.5	43.1
EBITDA	111.0	123.2	134.0	140.5	142.7

from realizing appropriate value for their interests in U.S. Can despite the company's good performance and has reduced the company's ability to provide effective stock-based incentives to employees. As a private company, U.S. Can will have the flexibility to focus on continuing improvements to its business without the constraints and distractions caused by the public market's present disfavor, despite strong underlying performance, for many "old economy" stocks such as U.S. Can. Each of the participating U.S. Can affiliates believes that the recapitalization represents an opportunity for you, as well as some of the rollover stockholders, to receive a substantial cash premium for your U.S. Can shares while also allowing the rollover stockholders to maintain at least a portion of their investment in U.S. Can. (Schedule 14-a, p. 30)

Omitted from the paragraph quoted is the desire for the senior management to have the opportunity to become richer.

The estimated fees and expenses to be incurred by U.S. Can in connection with the recapitalization are approximately as follows.

Advisory fees and expenses (1)	$ 7,550,000
Financing fees and expenses (2)	32,700,000
Legal fees and expenses (3)	4,000,000
Securities and Exchange Commission filing fees	55,267
Proxy solicitations, printing, and mailing costs	200,000
Total	$44,505,267

1. Includes the fees and expenses of Lazard, Salomon, Berkshire Partners, and other accounting and consulting fees and expenses.
2. Includes the fees and expenses of Bank of America, N.A. Banc of America Bridge LLC, Citibank, N.A., Banc of American Securities LLC, Salomon Smith Barney Inc., and bond tender expenses.
3. Includes the estimated fees and expenses of the respective legal counsel for U.S. Can, the special committee, and Pac.

Table 13.2 sets forth the estimated sources and uses of funds in connection with the transactions of July 2, 2000.

TABLE 13.2   Estimated Sources and Uses of Funds, July 2, 2000

Sources of Funds	(Dollars in millions)
New senior secured credit facility	
Revolving credit facility	$ 16.3
Term loans	260.0
Notes offered hereby	175.0
Preferred stock	106.7
Common stock	53.7
Available cash	2.0
Assumed debt	36.4
Total sources	$649.7

Uses of Funds	
Purchase capital stock	$276.0
Refinance existing debt	310.3
Payment of fees and expenses	26.1
Assumed debt	36.4
Total uses	$649.7

Table 13.3 sets forth as of July 2, 2000 the actual capitalization and the pro forma capitalization as adjusted to give effect to the transactions as if they had occurred on that date.

U.S. Can repurchased 32,195 shares during the first four months of 2000 at an average price of less than $18. F.A. Soler, a board member, bought 20,000 shares in the first four months of 2000 at an average price of $13.31. J.M. Kirk, a member of management, bought 5,000 shares at an average price of $13.75 (this seemed to be his initial investment in the company). G.V.N. Derbyshire, a member of management, bought 10,000 shares in the first four months of 2000 at an average price of $13.55.

Before the LBO there were 13,442,000 shares outstanding. The market capitalization is shown in Table 13.4.

A Partial LBO

Instead of an LBO we consider the consequences of a partial LBO strategy for U.S. Can.

TABLE 13.3   Capitalization and Pro Forma Capitalization

	As of July 2, 2000	
	Actual	Pro Forma Adjusted
	(Dollars in Millions)	
Cash and cash equivalents	$ 9.0	$ 7.0
Debt:		
Existing credit facility	$ 49.1	$ —
New senior secured facility		
Revolving credit facility	—	16.3
Term loans	—	260.0
Other senior debt	36.4	36.4
10⅛% senior subordinated notes due 2006	236.6	—
Notes offered hereby	—	175.0
Total debt	$322.1	$ 487.7
Preferred stock	$ —	$ 106.7
Stockholders' equity		
Common stock and additional paid-in capital	113.7	53.3
Treasury stock and unearned restricted stock	(2.1)	—
Current translation adjustment	(17.8)	(17.8)
Accumulated deficit	(22.9)	207.9
Total stockholders' equity (deficit)	$ 70.9	$ (172.4)
Total capitalization	$393.0	$ 422.0

TABLE 13.4   Market Capitalization

	Price of $15	Price of $20
	13,442,000	13,442,000
	× $15	× $20
	201,600,000	268,840,000
Management's ownership	.0054	.0054
Total	$1,090,000	$1,450,000

The pro-forma debt was $487.7 million and the actual debt was $322.1 million. Assume the $165.6 million of additional debt is used to buy 11,040,000 shares.

$$\frac{165,600,000}{15} = 11,040,000 \text{ shares}$$

There are initially 13,442,000 shares outstanding. After the share repurchase there will be 2,402,000 shares outstanding.

$$13,442,000 - 11,040,000 = 2,402,000 \text{ shares}$$

Management owns 72,590 shares. This was $\dfrac{72,590}{13,442,000} = .0054$

After the debt issuance and share repurchase management owns

$$\frac{72,590}{2,402,000} = .030$$

The First Year

Assume the cash flow from operations is $106 million, that maintenance cap-ex is $17 million, and that $89 million is available for share repurchase. The initial market capitalization is 13,442,000 ($15) = $201,600,000.

If the market cap at the end of year 1 is $201,600,000 − 165,000,000 + 58,000,000 = $94,000,000, this assumes the value added from debt issuance is $tB = .35(165.6) = \$58$ million.

With $89,000,000 of free cash being generated there is nearly enough to buy the $94,000,000 of outstanding common stock.

At the end of one year management would own nearly 100 percent of the stock (assuming they do not sell).

Using No Debt

Assume the market capitalization stays constant at $201,600,000.

$$13,442,000(\$15) = \$201,600,000$$

Also, assume that management is given 10 percent of the repurchased shares each year. Table 13.5 shows that there are 1,300,000 shares outstanding after four years.

TABLE 13.5   Shares Outstanding after Four Years

End of Year	Shares Outstanding	Price per Share	Shares Purchased with $89,000,000	New Number of Shares
1	13,442,000	$15.00	5,933,000	7,509,000
2	7,509,000	26.85	3,315,000	4,194,000
3	4,194,000	48.07	1,851,000	2,343,000
4	2,343,000	86.04	1,034,000	1,300,000

After four years management owns:

Initial ownership	72,590 shares
Year 1 award	593,000
Year 2 award	331,500
Year 3 award	185,100
Year 4 award	103,400
Total	1,285,890 shares

There are 1,300,000 shares outstanding so management owns .99 of the shares:

$$\frac{1,285,890}{1,300,000} = .99$$

The process could have been accelerated by the use of debt to finance more share repurchasing.

The partial LBO model works well with U.S. Can.

QUESTIONS AND PROBLEMS

1. What is happening to U.S. Can?

2. Who and what are the rollover stockholders?

3. What are the tax consequences of the transaction to the selling stockholders?

4. There is a one-time cash bonus of $1,182,700 for management. What do you think?

5. What percentage of equity will management own? What percentage of common equity?

6. If the total equity is $160 million after the recap, what is the value of management's investment? What was the value before the recap if management owned .54% of the equity?

7. How much were the total fees associated with the recapitalization?

8. What was the stock price on the last trading day before the recap announcement? What premium is being paid?

9. See the buying history. What do you think?

10. Assuming a market value of $15 per share and 13,442,000 shares what was the common stock's total value? With the earnings of $21,156,000 for 1999, what was P/E? What was the EPS?

11. The EBITDA for June 30, 2000 is $106.4 million. The ratio of market cap to EBITDA is what?

CHAPTER 14

Phillips Petroleum, Mesa, and Icahn (1984–1985)

This is a case of a failed acquisition and a successful restructuring. We can call this a partial LBO. The amount invested in the firm's common stock by the nonmanagement investors is greatly reduced by the restructuring.

Late in 1984 T. Boone Pickens through his firm Mesa Partners started to accumulate the common stock of Phillips Petroleum Corporation when the stock price was $40. By December 1984 Pickens and his partners had accumulated 8.9 million shares of Phillips stock. Mesa Partners then offered to buy as many as 23 million Phillips shares at a price of $60 per share. The Phillips stock price went up to $55 per share. There were then 154.6 million shares outstanding.

In January 1985 Phillips made an offer to Pickens and to the rest of its stockholders that caused Pickens to withdraw his offer. Phillips offered its common stockholders the following package:

- It would buy Mesa's 8.9 million shares of Phillips stock at $53 per share (Mesa did not have to accept).
- The remaining shareholders would receive:
    .62 of a common stock share
    $22.80 of debentures
- Stockholders would receive a dividend of $4.32 of preferred stock (145,000,000 shares).
- The common stock dividend of $2.40 per share would be maintained.

- The firm would tender 20,000,000 shares at $50 per share (the tender would be after the new shares were issued).
- The company's ESOP (Employee Stock Ownership Plan) would buy 24 million shares over the course of a year.

The $22.80 of debt consisted of the items listed in Table 14.1.

This package of cash and securities was rejected by the shareholders.

The offer was fought vigorously by Carl C. Icahn. The company valued the offer at $53 a share, but Icahn said that the recapitalization was worth only $42 a share. He offered an alternative plan where he would acquire the company's shares at $55 a share (the stockholders would receive an approximately equal amount of cash and securities).

Phillips attempted to stop the Icahn bid by legal means as well as by using a poison pill. The poison pill consisted of a right entitling each common stock to be swapped for $62 face amount of a 15 percent note. The right expired if the company's recapitalization plan was approved by the shareholders. The potential increase in debt was meant to discourage Icahn. By the end of February, Icahn had raised the price he was willing to pay to $60 per share for 70 million shares. The remainder of the shares (84.6 million shares) would be purchased at $50 a share using debt securities. After this offer the Phillips stock sold at about $48 per share. Phillips management was stating that the value per share was $62. On March 4, 1985, Phillips offered a new proposal that it said was worth in excess of $60.

- The company would buy Mesa's shares at $53 per share (Mesa did not have to accept). Mesa and Icahn each received $25,000,000 to cover their expenses.

TABLE 14.1 $22.80 of Debt

Amount	Interest
$11.00 of floating rate (initially .10) senior notes	$1.10
5.50 of .13 senior notes	.715
6.30 of .1375 subordinated debentures	.866
$22.80	$2.681

■ The shareholders who tendered would receive $4,500,000,000 of debentures in exchange for 72,580,000 shares. The debenture package was valued at $62 per share.

■ Stockholders would receive a dividend of $300,000,000 preferred stock (based on 73.1 million shares still outstanding after the purchase of 72.6 million shares; this would be worth $4.10 a share).

■ The common stock dividend of $2.40 would be increased to $3.00.

For each common stock share tendered, the debenture offer consisted of:

	Interest
$29 floating rate (currently paying .1125)	$3.2625
18 paying .13875	2.4975
15 paying .1475	2.2125
$62	$7.9725

Table 14.2 shows the two offers made by Phillips (assume there are initially 154.6 million shares outstanding).

TABLE 14.2 Summary of Phillips' Two Offers

	First Offer	Second Offer (72,600,000 Shares Exchanged)
Common Stocks	.62 of share for each old share	No shares offered
Debt	$22.80 per old share	$62 per share exchanged
Interest on debt	$2.68 per old share	$7.9725 per share exchanged
Dividend per share	$2.40 per new share	$3.00
Preferred stock		
145,700,000($3.32)	$484,000,000	
73,100,000($4.10)		$300,000,000
Stock repurchase (after restructuring): 20,000,000 shares @ $50 per share	$1,000,000,000	

ESOP buys 24,000,000 shares with the first offer.

The shares outstanding upon completion of the offers are shown in Table 14.3.

The second offer was accepted by the firm's shareholders and was executed by the firm. Note that the number of outstanding shares was reduced from 154.6 million to 73.1 million.

TABLE 14.3 Shares Outstanding and Stock Transactions

	First Offer	Second Offer
Initial shares	154.6	154.6
Pickens' shares retired	− 8.9	− 8.9
	145.7	145.7
Each share receives .62	× .62	−72.6
	90.3	73.1
Stock repurchase	−20.0	
Shares outstanding after repurchase	70.3	73.1

The financial facts for the two offers were:

	First Offer	Second Offer
Common stock shares (after repurchase)	70,300,000	73,100,000
Preferred stock	$ 484,000,000	$ 300,000,000
Debt		
145,700,000($22.80)	$3,322,000,000	
72,600,000($62)		$4,500,000,000
Stock repurchase (Financed with debt?)	$1,000,000,000	
Interest		
145,700,000($2.681)	$ 391,000,000	
1,000,000,000(.14)	140,000,000	
72,600,000($7.9725)		$ 579,000,000
	$ 531,000,000	$ 579,000,000
Common dividends		
70,300,000(2.40)	169,000,000	
73,100,000(3.00)		219,000,000
PS dividends (@ .10)	48,000,000	30,000,000
Total dividends	$ 217,000,000	$ 249,000,000
Stock repurchase	$1,000,000,000	

In a transaction such as this, management's percentage of ownership increases if:

■ Their stock options are rewritten for the same or a larger number of shares.
■ The ESOP has shares that are not exchanged for cash but are exchanged for new shares of common stock.
■ Management has shares that are not exchanged for cash, but are exchanged for new shares of common stock.

QUESTIONS AND PROBLEMS

1. Which of the facts given in the case are relevant in determining your preference of offers? How is value created?

2. Assuming an initial $40 stock price, what was the value of the stock equity before the restructuring?

3. Estimate the stock price per share after the second offer is accepted, and after the buyout of Mesa and after the three-for-one split.

4. The answers to (2) and (3) implicitly make what assumptions?

5. How much value per share does a shareholder receive from the second offer?

6. Carl Icahn demanded:

   ■ More preferred stock
   ■ Larger common stock dividend
   ■ A three for one stock split

   Of what economic significance are these changes?

7. If the first offer was worth $51.83 per share and the second offer was worth $52.39, what is the *total* value difference in the two offers?

8. Icahn and Pickens each received $25,000,000 to cover expenses. Is this ethical? Strategically sound?

9. Who won? Who lost?

CHAPTER 15

Owens–Corning Fiberglas Corporation (1986)

In the summer of 1986 Bill Boeschenstein and the other top executives of OCF could finally heave a sigh of relief. OCF's net income for 1985 was $131.2 million on stock equity of $944.7 million. The ROE of 14 percent was the best the firm had done since 1979. The years 1980 to 1983 had been difficult years and only since 1984 had the company made a return to acceptable profit performance. Best yet, the forecast was that 1986's operating results would be better than those of 1985. Finally, the firm's top management could plan on spending to diversify out of the building–construction industry and to modernize the production facilities. For 1987 the capital budget could be as high as $300 million. The long-term debt was a modest 36 percent of the total capital.

On August 12, 1986 the entire set of long range plans was placed in jeopardy. Wickes Acquisition I Inc. made a tender offer of $74 per share for any and all of OCF's common stock. The firm was a wholly owned subsidiary of Wickes Companies, Inc. The offer was to expire on September 9, 1986. The deal manager for the offer was Drexel Burnham Lambert. Drexel had the ability to raise debt capital (high yield, better known as junk bonds).

The financial history of Wickes is interesting and relevant. On January 25, 1984 Wickes had $1.3 billion of liabilities subject to reorganization proceedings and a stockholder deficit of $208 million. After reorganization Wickes eliminated the $1.3 billion of liabilities and had $992 of stockholders' equity as of April 24, 1986.

For the fiscal year ending January 26, 1985 Wickes had a net income of $297 million. Of this amount $281 million was the result of settlement of liabilities under the plan of reorganization and $16 million was the result of utilization of operating loss tax carryforwards. Wickes did make $28 million of income from continuing operations in the fiscal year ending January 25, 1986.

In 1986 Wickes issued (with the help of Drexel) $1.4 billion of 11⅞ percent senior subordinated debentures. The balance of funds needed to acquire OCF were to be obtained from private placements of debt and equity (again, Drexel) or from commercial banks. The company's statement was:

> In connection with the Offer, Wickes currently expects to privately place Senior Promissory Notes ("Senior Notes"), Increasing Rate Senior Notes ("Increasing Rate Notes"), Senior Convertible Debentures ("Convertible Debentures") and Cumulative Convertible Exchangeable Preferred Stock ("Exchangeable Preferred Stock") through Drexel Burnham. Drexel Burnham has informed Wickes that, based on current conditions, it is highly confident that it can obtain commitments for the private placement of up to $1.1 billion of such debt and equity securities of Wickes in connection with the Offer.

Wickes would obtain the capital based on OCF's debt capacity.

In his letter to OCF's shareholders Boeschenstein had stated (March 7, 1986):

> Looking ahead, we will continue to pursue our strategies for growth and enhanced profitability. Our plans and programs are designed to assure Owens–Corning's ability to compete successfully in all of its major markets, under varying economic conditions. We have made investments—in physical assets, technology and, most importantly, in people—to take advantage of our unique strengths and lay the foundation for future opportunities. We believe this is the best course for capitalizing on Owens–Corning's potential.

During the first half of 1986 the price of the OCF common stock ranged from $36 to $57. The projected incremental federal tax rate was .34.

OCF's management was shocked that a firm that had just come out of bankruptcy and that in its best most recent year had made one-fifth of OCF's operating income was trying to take over OCF. OCF intended to fight the offer.

OCF responded to the Wickes raid by offering its investors the following package:

- $52 of cash
- $35 of debentures with a market value of approximately $18
- 1 share of new common stock

The debentures mature in 20 years and accrue .15 interest starting December 1991 payable semi-annually starting June 1992. The .15 interest will be computed on the $35 face amount.

On August 29, 1986, after the announcement of OCF's proposed recapitalization, Wickes withdrew its offer of $74 per share in cash, for all the shares.

Goldman Sachs & Co., who acted as financial advisors to OCF in connection with the recapitalization, expressed an opinion in a "comfort letter" stating that "the aggregate consideration of $52 in cash, $35 stated face amount of debentures, and one new share to be received by the public stockholders, for each share of common stock held by them pursuant to the recapitalization is fair to the 'Public Stockholders.'" Note that Goldman did not value either the debentures or the new stock. Also, Goldman did not address the one way for the recapitalization to be unfair. It would be unfair to public shareholders if management received an excessively large number of options at a very favorable exercise price and received more than an appropriate percentage of the new shares.

There are initially 29,695,000 common shares outstanding. If all shares are exchanged, OCF will have to issue approximately $2,079 million of debt.

52(29,695,000)	$1,544,000,000
18(29,695,000)	535,000,000
	$2,079,000,000

Assuming a stock price of $50 before the start of the restructuring, the initial value of the unleveraged part of OCF is

$$V_U = 29,695,000(\$50) = \$1,485,000,000$$

Let $t_c = .34$ be the corporate tax rate and $B = \$2,079,000,000$ the amount of new debt. With the issuance of the new debt the new value of OCF is

$$
\begin{aligned}
V_L &= V_U + t_c B \\
&= 1,485,000,000 + .34(2,079,000,000) \\
&= 1,485,000,000 + 707,000,000 = \$2,192,000,000
\end{aligned}
$$

This calculation assumes the entire debt proceeds are given to the shareholders.

We want to determine the value of the stock equity. Assuming a distribution of $2,079,000,000 to stockholders and new debt of $2,079,000,000, we have

$$\text{Stock} = V_L - \text{Debt} = 2,192,000,000 - 2,079,000,000 = \$113,000,000$$

If all shares were exchanged, the new number of shares is 29,695,000. The new value per share is $3.81:

$$\text{Value per share} = \frac{113,000,000}{29,695,000} = \$3.81$$

This is only an estimate (an approximation) since the numerator can be increased by including gains in efficiency, thus further increasing the value per share. Also, not all shares will be exchanged for the package. Some shares controlled by management will be exchanged for new shares of common stock.

With the projected stock price of $3.81 (rounded to $4), and the value of a debenture rounded to $18, the total value received by a stockholder in exchange for one share of old stock is

Cash	$52
Debentures	18
Common stock	4
Value of package	$74

If the initial stock price were $57 rather than $50, the value of V_U would be $1,693,000,000 and the value with the issuance of $2,079,000,000 of debt is

$$V_L = 1,693,000,000 + 707,000,000 = \$2,400,000,000$$

and the value of the stock equity after the distribution of $2,079,000,000 to stockholders and the debt issuance is

$$V_L - \text{debt} = 2,400,000,000 - 2,079,000,000 = \$321,000,000$$

The new value per share is

$$\text{Value per share} = \frac{321,000,000}{29,695,000} = \$10.81$$

Now, rounding the $10.81 to $11.00 the shareholders receive in exchange for one share:

$$\text{Value received} = 52 + 18 + 11 = \$81$$

The $57 initial stock price is probably too high an estimate of value.

THE VALUE OF EXECUTIVE STOCK OPTIONS

Assume a corporate financial restructuring includes the substitution of debt for equity. This increase in leverage increases the risk to common stock (the variance of return on equity and the variance of earnings per share and the stock's beta) and thus, all things equal, the increase in leverage increases the value of outstanding stock options. The value of outstanding executive stock options is increased as the result of the substitution of debt for common stock if the debt proceeds are used to reduce the number of outstanding shares. We make the simplifying assumption that the Black–Scholes (1973) option pricing formula applies (if the options are issued by a firm paying a cash dividend, the formula does not apply exactly). While each financial restructuring is different, thus the option wealth effect is different, the substitution of debt for equity is a common element of restructurings. Also the form of the restructuring (cash dividends compared to share repurchase) can affect the value of an executive stock option even if the exercise price is kept equal to the stock price. The share repurchase alternative results in a higher stock price than with a cash dividend (of equal amount in total), thus increases the value of a stock option with a given exercise price.

The value of the option is increased by the increase in the standard deviation resulting from debt issuance, but the option value also depends on the share price after restructuring, which in turn depends on whether the debt amount is distributed in the form of a dividend or in the form of a share repurchase. The larger the share price, if the exercise price is kept constant, the larger the new option value.

Each outstanding option was adjusted by OCF to enable the holder to purchase 5.6 new common shares and the "exercise price will be adjusted accordingly." The adjustment to the exercise price was not revealed to the public.

Management (150 employees) were given the right to purchase 850,000 new common stock at fair market value. They were also awarded 1,400,000 new common shares (vested over five to seven years or less) and options to purchase 1,400,000 new common stock (exercise price equal to market price at date of grant). These options vest in five years or less.

As a result of all the above, management will control approximately 24.5 percent of the new common stock outstanding after the recapitalization. This is a larger percentage of ownership than many managements own after an LBO. Thus, we can call this transaction a partial LBO or a form of managerial buyout (MBO).

W.W. Boeschenstein before recapitalization had access to

122,684 shares (owned, options, and employee stock plan accounts). After the recapitalization he had access to 428,435 shares. Of course, the new shares had significantly less value per share than the old shares.

To be fair to the ESOP and comparable plans the company promised that the number of shares given will be equal to or exceed in value the value of a debenture plus $52 cash. Thus if the stock price is $15 after the Recapitalization, and the value of the debenture is $17, the ESOP would receive 4.6 new shares.

$$\frac{52 + 17}{15} = 4.6$$

It would also have the one old share, so it would have 5.6 shares.

As a result of the recapitalization long-term debt increased from $543 million (at the end of 1985) to $1,645 million (at the end of 1986). Current liabilities went from $548 million to $1,310 million. On the other hand, stock equity went from $945 million to a deficit of $1,025 million.

The OCF's net income was $131 million for 1985 and $16 million for 1986 (there were $200 million of restructuring costs and a $50 million increase in borrowing costs).

The stock of OCF prospered from 1986 to the late 1990s (with some ups and downs). For example, in 1992, it realized a low of $22 and a high of $40. Unfortunately, in the year 2000 asbestos liabilities grew exponentially and the company entered bankruptcy.

CONCLUSIONS

Corporate restructurings where there are managerial stock options outstanding typically lead to a change in the value of the managerial stock options. Among the important decision variables are:

■ Whether the cash from the debt issuance is distributed to the shareholders in the form of a dividend or a share repurchase (the expected stock price is affected)

■ The amount of debt issued in substitution for common stock
■ The exercise price
■ The maturity date of the options
■ The number of options granted

Since the value of the managerial stock options is greatly affected by the above decision variables, it is very important that the shareholders understand the option value implications of the restructuring. Any restructuring prospectus should contain this information.

In a restructuring situation, the total value of the new options can be equated to the total value of the initial options by changing the number of new options and the exercise prices.

The fact that a corporate restructuring with debt substituted for stock leads to a change in the value of managerial stock options has been information that has not been presented to shareholders voting on various plans. The different values of the managerial stock options for the different alternatives should be available to shareholders. Any restructuring prospectus should contain the information.

When debt is issued and the relationship $V_L = V_U + t_c B$ is applied, it must be remembered that it is implicitly assumed that all the debt issued is being substituted for common stock. The value of the new stock is: $S = V_L -$ debt issued.

While it would be surprising if the stock price after the restructuring exactly equaled the value computed applying the formulas of this chapter (because of other changes that are taking place), the calculations help us estimate the magnitude of the new stock price.

The preceding formulas cannot be used as presented if the debt's proceeds are retained by the corporation.

QUESTIONS AND PROBLEMS

1. Should Mr. Boeschenstein accept the Wickes offer?

2. What is the value of the $35 debenture (assume a .15 discount rate)?

3. Assume the initial stock price is $50 and there are 29,695,000 shares outstanding initially. There are 347,000 shares in the ESOP that will not be exchanged (they will receive a number of new shares). There will be 29,348,000 shares exchanged and receiving $52 cash, a debenture (see 2), and a new share of stock. To finance the restructuring, $2,037,000,000 of debt will be issued. Assume 30,000,000 shares will be outstanding after the exchange. What will be the new stock value after the exchange?

4. What is the value of the distribution to a shareholder if the investment banker's plan is accepted? Use the information from questions (2) and (3).

5. If the investment banker's plan is accepted what real things should OCF management then do?

6. How can management turn this negative event (a raid by Wickes) into a positive event?

7. If the firm guarantees that the ESOP will receive as much value as the shareholders receive who exchange, what will be the new stock price if the new stock equity value is $141,000,000 after the exchange?

Solutions

solutions

CHAPTER 1   The Many Virtues of Private Equity

1. Simplicity (information)

    Alignment of management and ownership

    Eliminates dividend policy conflicts

    Allows more debt

    Eliminates the quarterly target for income compulsion

2. This is a matter of taste. Probably potential improvements in managerial incentives but tax savings are also important. See answer to question 1.

3. The interest expense is $5.60.

    The taxable income is $90 - 5.60 = 84.40$. The tax is $.35(84.40) = 29.54$.

    The income net of tax is $90 - 29.54 = \$60.46$. The allocation is:

Taxes	$29.54
Management (.02)	2.00
.20(60.46)	12.09
Interest (.14)	5.60
Preferred (.12)	3.60
Convertible (.06)	1.20
Subtotal	$54.03
Return to equity	35.97
Total	$90.00

4. Taxable income = 45 − 5.60 = 39.40

Tax = .35(39.40) = 13.79

Income net of tax = 45 −13.79 = $31.21

The allocation is:

Tax	$13.79
Management	
100(.02)	2.00
.20(31.21)	6.24
Interest (.14)	5.60
Preferred (.12)	3.60
Convertible (.06)	1.20
Subtotal	$32.43
Return to equity	12.57
Total	$45.00

A 50 percent reduction in before tax income reduces the equity return from $35.97 to $12.57.

CHAPTER 2   Valuing the Target Firm

1. The present value calculation requires a forecast of the future. The market capitalization requires only the market price of a share and the number of shares outstanding. Is the market price reliable?

2. The firm is writing-off to expense a large amount of intangibles or tangible long-lived assets.

   The firm has extra cash or the equivalent.

   The firm has abnormal liabilities.

   The firm has a special tax status (e.g., it is a partnership).

   The earnings are abnormally high or low.

3. A low retention rate (b) and a large growth rate (g) implies the firm has good reinvestment opportunities (r).

   It is reasonable to expect a high P/E ratio.

4. EBITDA times a multiplier is likely to give the total firm value. To obtain the equity value one must subtract the value of the outstanding debt.

5. Since

$$b = .6 \text{ and } g = .10$$
$$g = rb$$
$$.10 = .6r$$
$$r = .1667$$
$$.4E = 50$$
$$E = \$125$$
$$2,500 = \frac{E}{k} + PVGO = \frac{125}{.12} + PVGO$$
$$PVGO = \$1,458$$

Also

$$PVGO = \frac{E(g - bk)}{k(k - g)} = \frac{125[.10 - .6(.12)]}{.12(.12 - .10)}$$

$$= \frac{3.5}{.0024} = \$1,458$$

CHAPTER 3   Structuring and Selling the Deal

1. Corporations get a 70 percent (or more) dividend received deduction that is not available for individuals.

2a. Max new debt $= \dfrac{S}{1-t} = \dfrac{6,500,000}{1-.35} = \$10,000,000$

2b. Net = 10,000,000 – 7,000,000 = $3,000,000

2c. $\$7,000,000(1 + IRR)^4 = \$12,243,000$

$$IRR = .150$$

2d. The debt pays $6,000,000(1.8)^4 = 8,162,900$

$1,000,000 = (12,243,000 - 8,162,900)(1 + IRR)^4$

$1,000,000(1 + IRR)^4 = 12,243,000 - 8,162,900 = 4,080,100$

$IRR = .421$

2e.

Time	Debt	Interest (.08)	Tax Savings	End of Period
0	6,000,000	480,000	168,000	1
1	6,480,000	518,400	181,440	2
2	6,998,400	559,872	195,955	3
3	7,558,272	604,662	211,632	4

Future value $= 211,632 + 195,955(1.052) + 181,440(1.052)^2$
$$+\ 168,000(1.052)^3$$
$$= 211,632 + 206,145 + 200,800 + 195,594$$
$$= 814,171$$

Add $814,171 to $4,080,000 = $4,894,271

2f. $1,000,000(1 + IRR)^4 = 4,894,271$

$$IRR = .487$$

3. $1,000,000(1.30)^4 = \$2,856,100$

CHAPTER 4   A Changed Dividend Policy

1a. After tax dividend = $(1 - .396)\$100 = \$60.40$

$60.40(1.07248)^{20} = \$244.81$

1b. $100(1.12)^{20} = \$964.63$

$$\underline{\times .8}$$

After tax = $\$771.70$ (compare with $\$244.81$)

2. $60.40(1 + IRR)^{20} = 771.70$

$$IRR = .1358$$

3a. $P = \dfrac{(1 - .396)100}{.07248} = \$833.33$

3b. $PV = (7,205.24 - 1,441.05)(1.07248)^{-20} + 833.33(1.07248)^{-20}$

$= 1,422.18 + 205.60 = \$1,627.78$ (compare with $\$833.33$)

CHAPTER 5 A Changed Capital Structure

1.

	0	1	IRR
	−800	+1,000	.25
	+700	−756	.08
Equity	−100	+244	1.44 or 144%

2a. $V_L = V_U + tB$

$= 1,000 + .35(800) = 1,000 + 280 = \$1,280$

$S = V_L - B = 1,280 - 800 = \$480$

Wealth $= 480 + 800 = \$1,280$

2b. Interest $= (.10)800 = 80$ Tax saving $= .35(80) = \$28$

$$PV = \frac{28}{.10} = \$280$$

3a. $(1 - .35)1,000 = \$650$

3b.
Stock return $= (1,000 - 720)(1 - .35)$	\$182
Debt return $= .65(720)$	468
Total return	\$650

3c. The returns are equal.

3d.
Stock return $= (2,000 - 720)(.65)$	832
Debt return $= .65(720)$	468
Total return	\$1,300

$2,000(.65) = \$1,300$ all stock

4.
Stock return $= (2,000 - 900)(.65)$	715
Debt return $= .65(900)$	585
Total return	\$1,300

$2,000(.65) = \$1,300$ all stock

$$\text{Net} = 60.40[(1.10)^{20} - .20[(1.10)^{20} - 1)]]$$
$$= 60.40[6.7275 - .20(5.7275)]$$
$$= 60.40(5.582) = \$337$$

The taxes imposed on the two strategies are different.

We can expect there to be a wide range of estimates of the expected value of the costs of financial distress and the expected value of tax savings from debt interest as well as the other factors associated with the debt issuance, thus a large difference of opinion as to how much debt a firm should issue in substitution for equity.

The returns do not depend on the interest rates, given the investment strategies.

5. $$k_o = k_o(0)\left[1 - t\frac{B}{V_L}\right]$$

$$V_L = V_U + tB = 1,000 + .35(900) = 1,315$$

$$k_o = .12\left[1 - \frac{.35(900)}{1,315}\right] = .0913$$

6. ■ $$V_L = \text{max debt} = \frac{V_U}{1-t} = \frac{10,000,000}{1-.35} = \$15,385,000$$

   ■ Value added = \$15,385,000 −10,000,000 = \$5,385,000

7a.

1	2	IRR
10,000	+10,900	.09
+ 9,000	− 9,450	.05
− 1,000	+ 1,450	.45

7b. ■ Taxable income = 12,000 − 10,000 − 450 = $1,550

Tax = .35(1,550) = $542.50

Net = 12,000 − 542.50 = $11,457.50

Interest	$ 450.00
Debt	9,000.00
Net	$2,007.50

$$IRR = \frac{11,300}{10,000} - 1 = 1.0075 \text{ or } 100.75\%$$

■ Tax = .35(12,000 − 10,000) = 700

Net = 12,000 − 700 = 11,300

$$IRR = \frac{11,300}{10,000} - 1 = .13 \text{ or } 13\%$$

8a. $V_L = V_U + tB$

$V_L = 10,000,000 + .35(8,000,000) = \$12,800,000$

$S = V_L - B = 12,800,000 - 8,000,000 = \$4,800,000$

8b. Wealth = $12,800,000 (stock plus debt).

8c. No change.

Present value of tax savings = $\dfrac{tk_i B}{k_i} = tB$

where k_i = the debt cost

8d. $k_o = k_o(0)\left[1 - t\dfrac{B}{V_L}\right]$

$$= .15\left[1 - .35\left(\frac{8}{12.8}\right)\right] = .1172$$

8e. $k_o = .15[1 - .35] = .0975$ if $B = V_L$

CHAPTER 6 Merchant Banking

1a. $P_o = \dfrac{(1-t_p)D}{r_p} = \dfrac{(1-.396)8}{.12} = \$40.27$

1b. $P_o = \$40.27$ (same as question 1)

1c. $P_o = (1 - t_p)D\ B(n,r_p) + t_g P_o(1.12)^{-n}$

$P_o = 4.832\ B(20,.12) + .2P_o(1.12)^{-20}$

$P_o = 36.09735 + .0273P_o$

$P_o = \$36.86$

2. $PV = -(100.20 - 40.27).2(1.07248)^{-5} + 100.20(1.07248)^{-5}$

$\quad = 70.62 - 8.45 = \$62.17$

CHAPTER 8   The Many Virtues of Going Public

1. Advantages of a publicly traded stock:

   ■ Liquidity
   ■ Well defined price
   ■ Impersonal market
   ■ Simplification of control issues
   ■ Diversification for owners
   ■ Capital raising facilitated
   ■ Can attract management with options
   ■ Merger premium

2a. $PV = \dfrac{2,538(1-.2)+604}{(1.12)^{10}} = \dfrac{2,634.4}{3.1058} = \$848$

2b. $604(1 + IRR)^{10} = 2,634.4$

$$IRR = .159$$

CHAPTER 9   A Partial LBO: Almost Private Equity

1a. $\dfrac{100,000,000 - 10,000,000}{20} = 4,500,000$ shares

1b.

Year	Shares Outstanding	V = $400,000,000 Price per Share	Shares Purchased with $90,000,000	Percentage of Ownership
1	20,000,000	20.00	4,500,000	25%
2	15,500,000	25.81	3,488,000	32%
3	12,012,000	33.30	2,703,000	42%
4	9,309,000	42.97	2,095,000	54%
5	7,214,000			69%

CHAPTER 10   Metromedia (1984)

1. Serial zero-coupon ($960 nominal) $ 380
   15-year debentures   225
   12-year exchangeable   335
   18-year floating rate   400

   Total $1,358

2. Assume 29,584,000 shares outstanding in 1983.

   Purchase price = 40.16(29,584,000) = $1,188,000,000

   $$\text{Premium} = \frac{40.16}{35.75} - 1 = .123 \text{ Using high for quarter}$$

   $$\text{Premium} = \frac{40.16}{20.38} - 1 = .971 \text{ Using low for year}$$

   Debt offering $1,358
   Tax rate   × .46
   Value added $ 625

   Assume
   $V_U = $20.38(29,584,000) $ 602,922,000
   tB +   625,000,000
   V_L $1,227,922,000

   V_L exceeds the amount paid for the stock.

3. The premium being paid over price ranged from .123 to .971 (see above). The $40 offer price is reasonable but not as good as could be earned if the company restructured (both assets and capital structure).

   For example, the cash dividend could be eliminated without an LBO. Debt could be issued.

   Pieces of the firm could be sold (get a focus).

4. ■ *tB*
   ■ Sale of pieces at good prices
   ■ Focus

5. Add an equity kicker.

6. 20.38(29,584,000) = $602,922,000
   $$\frac{\times\ .26}{\$156,800,000}$$

7. V_L = 1,228,000,000

   B = 1,358,000,000

   S = Negative. The equity value is the value of an option.

   Different results are obtained if $40.16 is used as the stock price to obtain V_U.

V_U = 40.16(29,584,000)	$1,188,093,000
tB	+ 625,000,000
V_L	$1,813,093,000
B	−1,358,000,000
S	$ 455,093,000

CHAPTER 11   LBO of RJR Nabisco (1988)

1. $V_L = V_U + tV_L$

$$V_L = \frac{V_U}{1-t}$$

With $V_U = \$50(233 \text{ million shares}) = \$11.65$ billion

$$V_L = \frac{11.65}{12-.34} = \$17.65 \text{ billion}$$

2. EBITDA = $1,840 + 682 = 2,522$ million

where 682 = the tax paid

$$\text{Debt} = \frac{2,522}{.12} = \$21.017 \text{ billion}$$

or

$.34Y = 682$

$Y = \$2.006$ billion where Y is the taxable income

$$\text{Debt} = \frac{2.006}{.12} = \$16.72 \text{ billion}$$

$$V_L = \frac{V_U}{1-t} = \frac{(1-t)X}{(1-t)k_{e(0)}} = \frac{X}{k_{e(0)}}$$

If $k_e(0) = .12$

$$V_L = \frac{2,522}{.12} = \$21.017 \text{ billion}$$

A higher interest rate would reduce the debt capacity.

3. 233 million shares outstanding
   $\times \$109$ price
   $\$25,397$ million or $\$25.397$ billion. Purchase price.

4. Compare $25.397 billion with any of the above calculations.

$$P/E = \frac{25.397}{1.378} = \$18.43 \qquad \text{This is large.}$$

KKR overpaid; KKR won the bid but paid too much.

CHAPTER 12   Marietta Corporation (1994–1996)

Valuation of Marietta
(September 30, 1995)

1. Using the balance sheet:

Current assets	$32,300,000
Restricted cash	2,700,000
Marketable securities	2,400,000
Total cash equivalents	$37,400,000
Current liabilities	8,600,000
Net cash equivalents	$28,800,000

How much could be captured?

There was $6,500,000 of long-term debt.

Debt and Value

Net long-term debt (book) $6,514,000

Assume cost was .06 over 12 years.

$$\text{Equal annual payment} = \frac{6,514,000}{B(12,.06)} = \frac{6,514,000}{8.3838} = \$777,000$$

$$\begin{aligned} PV \text{ using } .10 &= 777,000\ B(12,.10) \\ &= 777,000(6.8137) \\ &= \$5,300,000 \end{aligned}$$

Reduction in liability = $1,200,000

2. Estimating the value

Quarter Ending December 30, 1995

Net income	$ 400,000
Taxes	300,000
Depreciation*	800,000
Goldman*	300,000
EBITDA for quarter	$ 1,800,000
Annualized	× 4
EBITDA	$ 7,200,000
Multiplier	× 4
	$28,800,000
Balance sheet values	28,800,000
Value of firm	$57,600,000

$$\text{Per share} = \frac{57,600,000 - 5,300,000}{3,621,000} = \$14.44$$

Is the quarter's performance average for the year?

Using Net Income	$ 400,000
	× 4
Annual Income	$ 1,600,000
	× 10
Total stock value	$16,000,000 or $2.76 per share
(add the balance sheet value)	

LBO Value

Using 1995's lowest price:

$V_U = 3{,}621{,}000(\$8.00)$	$29,000,000
Add $40,000,000 of debt	
× .35	$14,000,000
V_L	$43,000,000**

---

*Estimated
**Before balance sheet values of $28,800,000

Can change the amount of debt and initial stock price

$$P = \frac{43,000,000}{3,621,000} = \$11.88$$

$$P = \frac{43 + 28.8}{3.621} = \$19.83$$

Using a price of $8.

$V_U = 3,621,000(\$8.00)$	$28,968,000
tB	14,000,000
Cash, and so on	28,800,000
	$71,768,000

$$P = \frac{71.768}{3.621} = \$19.82$$

3. Is $40,000,000 of .10 debt feasible?

   $4,000,000 of interest with $7,200,000 of EBITDA is feasible. Some of the debt could be zero coupon.

   NOTE: $10.25(3,621,000) = $37,115,000

4. A share repurchase program that used excess liquid assets and debt capacity would have interesting effects on the stock price.

CHAPTER 13 The Managerial Buyout of United States Can Company (2000)

1. This is an MBO (or LBO). A merger with Pac. A $20 per share tender offer

2. Who? Management, directors, and their affiliates

   What? Keep or increase their shares in U.S. Can

3. A capital gain

4. The bonus goes to management. I would not like to invest in a firm with management fleeing. The bonus is not tax efficient. Is it a bribe? An incentive?

5. 9% of common and 3% of total equity

6. .03($160) = $4.8 million

   Value before recap = $1.45 million (.54% of equity) with a $20 price per share and $1.09 million with a $15 price per share

7. Total fees were $44.5 million.

8. The low was $14.562 and the high was $15.00

   $$\text{Premium} = \frac{20}{15} - 1 = .333$$

9. Suspect
   Buying by U.S. Can in 2000
   Buying by Derbyshire in 2000
   Buying by Kirk in 2000
   Buying by Soler in 2000

10. 13,442,000($15) = $201,600,000

$$P/E = \frac{201,600,000}{21,156,000} = 9.5$$

$$EPS = \frac{21,156,000}{13,442,000} = \$1.57$$

11. $\dfrac{201.6}{106.4} = 1.89$

CHAPTER 14   Phillips Petroleum, Mesa, and Icahn (1984–1985)

1. The different amounts of debt are relevant. Value is added here by increasing the amount of debt.

2. $V_U = 40(154,600,000) = \$6,184,000,000$
$V_L = V_U + tB = 6,184,000,000 + .46(4,500,000,000)$
$\quad = 6,184,000,000 + 2,070,000,000 = \$8,254,000,000$
Value added $= 8,254,000,000 - 6,184,000,000$
$\quad\quad\quad\quad = \$2,070,000,000$

3. SE value after buyout of Mesa

V_L		$\$8,254,000,000$
less		
Debt	$\$4,500,000,000$	
Mesa	$472,000,000$	
P stock	$300,000,000$	
Mesa & Icahn	$50,000,000$	
Trans. Costs	$100,000,000$	$5,422,000,000$
SE		$\$2,832,000,000$

E value per share $= \dfrac{2,832}{73.1} = \$38.74$

Stock split $\dfrac{38.74}{3} = \$12.91$

4. Assumptions:
   - ■ Perpetuity of tax savings
   - ■ Constant tax rate
   - ■ All tax shields can be used
   - ■ No costs of financial distress
   - ■ Market believes the first four.

5. Second offer

Debt: $\quad\$62 \times \dfrac{72.6}{145.7}\qquad\qquad \$30.89$

CS: $\quad\$38.74 \times \dfrac{73.1}{145.7}\qquad\qquad 19.44$

PS: $\quad\dfrac{300,000,000}{145,700,000}\qquad\qquad \underline{2.06}$

$$\$52.39$$

Assuming holding stockholders receive preferred.

Mesa receives

$$\dfrac{472+25}{8.9} = \$55.84 \text{ gross or } \dfrac{472}{8.9} = \$53.00 \text{ net}$$

6. Evaluation of Icahn's Changes

Preferred Stock

Without preferred stock: Common stockholders receive: Y

With preferred stock paying D_p: Common stockholders owning the preferred stock receive:

$$(Y - D_p) + D_p = Y$$

Increased Dividend

Let S = basic value of common stock exclusive of dividend

RE = value of retention

With dividend: Value = $S + (1 - t_p)D$

Without dividend: Value = $S + RE$ where RE is value of retained earnings

Which is better?

Stock split

A 3-for-1 stock split increases the number of shares threefold, and reduces the price per share by two-thirds; the overall value of the stock is unchanged.

None of the changes add value.

Preferred Stock Given to Common Stockholders

With common stock earning X and no preferred stock the investor earns an ROI of

$$r = \frac{X}{Inv}$$

With P of preferred paying k_p given to the common, investor earns

$$r(Inv) = (k_p P) + \frac{(X - k_p P)}{S} S$$
$$= (k_p P) + X - (k_p P) = X$$

or

dividing by Inv:

$$r = \frac{X}{Inv}$$

The ROI is independent of k_p and P.

Total earnings: X

100% Common: Investor earns X

P of preferred stock given to common. Preferred pays dividend of Div. Investor earns:

X – div. on preferred

$\underline{\quad + \text{div. on preferred}}$

$X \qquad\qquad\quad$ total

Total earnings are not affected.

7. Second offer	$	52.39
First offer		51.83
Difference		.56
Number of shares		145,700,000
Change in value	$	81,900,000
Debt: Second offer		$4,500,000,000
Debt: First offer		4,322,000,000
Increase in debt		178,000,000
		× .46
Change in value $(t_c B)$	$	81,900,000

8. Ethical? Not particularly.

   Strategic? Accomplished objective.

9. Won:

   ■ Shareholders
   ■ Management stays in place
   ■ Pickens, Icahn (sold stock at a gain)

   Lost:

   ■ Workers
   ■ Tax collector
   ■ Management
   ■ Bondholders

CHAPTER 15   Owens–Corning Fiberglas Corporation (1986)

1. Wickes offered $74 per share for all shares. How would Wickes finance the purchase? Using OCF's debt capacity. A fair offer but insulting to management.

2. Value of $35 debenture

   Will mature on December 1, 2006 and pay $35.
   Time till maturity—20 years
   No interest paid until June 1, 1992 (5½ years)
   15% per annum, paid semiannually. Callable

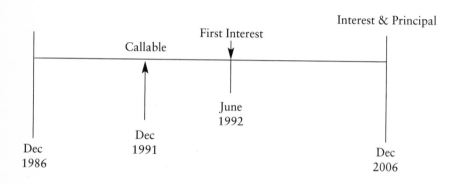

   Using .15 as the discount rate:

   PV at Dec. 1991 = $35

   PV of Dec. 1986 = 35(1.15)$^{-5}$ = 35(.4972) = $17.40

3. $29{,}348{,}000 \times \$52$ $\$1{,}526{,}000{,}000$ Cash distribution
    $29{,}348{,}000 \times 17.40$ $\underline{511{,}000{,}000}$ Debentures

New Debt	$\$2{,}037{,}000{,}000^{*}$
t_c	$\underline{.34}$
$t_c B$	$693{,}000{,}000$

$V_U = 50(29{,}695{,}000)$	$\underline{1{,}485{,}000{,}000}$
V_L	$2{,}178{,}000{,}000$
B	$\underline{-2{,}037{,}000{,}000}$
S	$141{,}000{,}000^{**}$

$$\text{New price} = \frac{141{,}000{,}000}{30{,}000{,}000} = \$4.70$$

4. Stockholders receive:

Cash	$\$52.00$
Debenture	17.40
Stock	$\underline{4.70}$
Value	$\$74.10$

5. Possible actions:

- Sell business.
- Sell assets.
- Eliminate products.
- Reduce channels of distribution.
- Eliminate excess capacity (mothball).
- Reduce and change capital expenditures.
- Retire people.

---

*The severance pay will also require debt.
**Can be increased by operating efficiencies.

6. ■ Receive stock options.
   ■ Receive new shares for old shares owned by management.
   ■ Have the ESOP receive new shares for old shares (the ESOP is controlled by management).

7. Let n be the shares given to the ESOP for each share initially owned (347,000) and P be the new share value.

   I $52 + 17.40 + P = nP$

   II $29,348,000P + nP(347,000) = 141,000,000$

   Solving I for P:

   $$P = \frac{69.40}{n-1}$$

   II $29,348,000\dfrac{69.40}{n-1} + n(347,000)\dfrac{69.40}{n-1} = 141,000,000$

   Solving for n:

   $$29,348,000 + 347,000n = 2,032,000(n-1)$$
   $$31,380,000 = 1,685,000n$$
   $$n = 18.623$$

   $$P = \frac{69.40}{18.623-1} = \$3.938$$

   Value $= 18.623(\$3.938) = \$73.34$

   Shares outstanding $= 29,348,000 + 18.623(347,000)$
   $$= 29,348,000 + 6,462,000$$
   $$= 35,810,000 \text{ shares}$$

   Redoing the answer to (3)

   New price $= \dfrac{141,000,000}{35,000,000} = \$3.94$

Stockholders who exchange receive value of:

Cash	$52.00
Debentures	17.40
Stock	3.94
Total	$73.34

The ESOP receives the same value.

On August 5, 1986, the day OCF was advised of Wickes' interest, the closing sales price for the common shares was $74.

references

Allen, J. "Reinventing the Corporation: The Satellite Structure of Thermo Electron," *Journal of Applied Corporate Finance.* Summer 1998, pp. 38–47.

Asquith, P. and T.A. Wizman. "Event Risk, Covenants, and Bondholder Returns in Leveraged Buyouts," *Journal of Financial Economics.* September 1990, pp. 195–214.

Baker, G.P. "Beatrice: A Study in the Creation and Destruction of Value," *Journal of Finance.* July 1992, pp. 1,081–1,120.

Black, F. and M. Scholes. "The Pricing of Options and Corporate Liabilities," *Journal of Political Economy* 81 (1993), pp. 637–659.

Brealey, R.A. and S.C. Myers. *Principles of Corporate Finance.* Boston: Irwin, McGraw-Hill, 2000.

Burrough, B. and J. Helya. *Barbarians at the Gate*, New York: Harper & Row, 1970.

DeAngelo, H. and L. DeAngelo. "Management Buyouts of Publicly Traded Corporations," T.E. Copeland, *Modern Finance & Industrial Economics.* New York: Blackwell, 1987, pp. 92–113.

DeAngelo, H., L. DeAngelo, and E.M. Rice. "Going Private: Minority Freeze-outs and Stockholder Wealth," *Journal of Law and Economics.* October 1984, pp. 307–401.

DeAngelo, H., L. DeAngelo, and E.M. Rice. "Going Private: The Effects of a Change in Corporate Ownership Structures," *Midland Corporate Finance Journal.* Summer 1994, pp. 35–43.

Diamond, S.C. *Leveraged Buyouts.* Homewood, Illinois: Dow Jones–Irwin, 1985.

Jensen, M.C. "Agency Costs of Free Cash Flow, Corporate Finance, and Takeovers," *American Economic Review*. May 1986, pp. 323–329.

Jensen, M.C. "Corporate Control and the Politics of Finance," *The New Corporate Finance*. Edited by D.H. Chew, Jr., New York: McGraw-Hill, Inc., 1993, pp. 620–640.

Jensen, M.C. "The Eclipse of the Public Corporation," *Harvard Business Review*. September/October 1989, pp. 61–74.

Jensen, M.C. and W.H. Meckling. "Theory of the Firm: Management Behavior, Agency Costs and Ownership Structure," *Journal of Financial Economics*. October 1976, pp. 305–360.

Kaplan, S.N. "The Effect of Management Buyouts on Operating Performance and Value," *Journal of Financial Economics*. October 1989, pp. 217–254.

Kaplan, S.N. "The Staying Power of Leveraged Buyouts," *Journal of Applied Corporate Finance*. Spring 1993, pp. 15–24.

Kaplan, S.N. and J.C. Stein. "The Evolution of Buyout Pricing and Financial Structure (or What Went Wrong) in the 1980's," *Journal of Applied Corporate Finance*. Spring 1993, pp. 72–88.

Kleiman, R.T. "The Shareholder Gains from Leveraged Cash-Outs: Some Preliminary Evidence," *Journal of Applied Corporate Finance*. Spring 1988, pp. 46–53.

Megginson, W.L., R.C. Nash, and M. vanRadenburgh. "The Record on Privatization," *Journal of Applied Corporate Finance*. Spring 1996, pp. 23–34.

Michel, A. and I. Shaked. "RJR Nabisco: A Case Study of a Complex Leveraged Buyout," *Financial Analysts Journal*. September–October 1991, pp. 15–27.

Miller, M.H. and F. Modigliani. "Dividend Policy, Growth and the Valuation of Shares," *The Journal of Business*. University of Chicago, October 1961, pp. 411–433.

Stern, J.M. and D.H. Chew, Jr. *The Revolution in Corporate Finance*. Malden, Mass.: Blackwell, 1998, pp. 351–444.

Weston, J.F., J.A. Siu, and B.A. Johnson. *Takeovers, Restructuring,*

& *Corporate Governance.* Upper Saddle River, N.J.: Prentice-Hall, 2001.

Wruck, K.H. "What Really Went Wrong at Revco," *The New Corporate Finance.* Edited by D.H. Chew, Jr., New York: McGraw-Hill, Inc., 1993, pp. 654–667.

index